PENGUIN BOOKS

# the caribbean cook

For two years, Patrick Williams was Head Chef at Greens Champagne and Oyster Bar in London. He has since worked for Marco Pierre White at the Criterion and Titanic. He has co-presented *Hey Pesto* and *Four Burners and a Grill* for cable television. He is a regular chef on *Lorraine Live* on Sky One and co-presented BBC2's *Planet Christmas* in December 2001. He lives in London.

# the caribbean cook

Patrick Williams

PENGUIN BOOKS

PENGUIN BOOKS

Published by the Penguin Group
Penguin Books Ltd, 80 Strand, London WC2R 0RL, England
Penguin Putnam Inc., 375 Hudson Street, New York, New York 10014, USA
Penguin Books Australia Ltd, 250 Camberwell Road, Camberwell,
Victoria 3124, Australia
Penguin Books Canada Ltd, 10 Alcorn Avenue, Toronto, Ontario, Canada M4V 3B2
Penguin Books India (P) Ltd, 11 Community Centre, Panchsheel Park,
New Delhi – 110 017, India
Penguin Books (NZ) Ltd, Cnr Rosedale and Airborne Roads,
Albany, Auckland, New Zealand
Penguin Books (South Africa) (Pty) Ltd, 24 Sturdee Avenue,
Rosebank 2196, South Africa

Penguin Books Ltd, Registered Offices: 80 Strand, London WC2R 0RL, England

www.penguin.com

First published by Michael Joseph 2001
Published in Penguin Books 2003
1

Set in Monotype Grotesque Light
Printed and bound in Spain by AGT Toledo

# contents

vii | *Introduction*

1 | Breakfast

11 | Soups

19 | Salads

35 | Snacks

47 | Vegetables

73 | Seafood

89 | Meat

105 | For the Barbie

113 | Rice, Pulses, Noodles and Grains

123 | Puddings and Cakes

141 | Drinks

157 | Stocks, Sauces, Salsas and Dressings

193 | *Glossary*

199 | *Acknowledgements*

201 | *Index*

# introduction

As an only child growing up in a West Indian household, with a mother as ruthless as Blackbeard, I was very quickly trained in domestic life. This was especially true of cooking and cleaning and other chores a young boy thought he shouldn't be doing. Out of all these things I came to enjoy cooking and eating. Some of my fondest memories revolve around the tastes and smells of the kitchen. Thinking back always brings a smile to my face as I remember family squabbles around the dinner table which would usually end in me being told off for being too greedy.

Whether it was a traditional Jamaican breakfast such as ackee and saltfish with breadfruit and cerassie tea, or one of my favourite soups, like oxtail or butter bean, there was always something interesting on our family table. Trips to my aunts' and uncles' houses were eagerly anticipated, as I found most of them to be wizards in the kitchen, conjuring up a variety of new things at the drop of a hat and most of the time from surprisingly few ingredients. Between my family and watching the Galloping Gourmet on TV, a chef was born.

Although my formal training has mostly been classic French, I've always looked at the ways in which West Indian food could benefit from the techniques of French cooking – and vice versa. I've spent the last few years picking the brains of my parents and grandparents about the dishes they were brought up on in the West Indies, and the produce not available in Britain. I've travelled to the Caribbean to research the local food and spent time with fishermen and farmers, learning how to cook their harvest. I've eaten the most wonderful crab and mango salad and jerk chicken possible.

Most of the books I've read on Caribbean cooking have, on the whole, been very basic. Instead of concentrating on the more traditional dishes, in this book I'd like to create my own Caribbean style that will appeal to everyone. You may feel you want to experiment with this sort of food but need a bit of direction. Maybe you are looking for a more modern style of Caribbean food with a slicker presentation but one which is faithful to the characteristic flavours. In either case, I will draw on my culinary skills to take you to the Caribbean and evoke images of sitting on a beach eating fresh fish washed down with guava juice. There is an abundance of produce in Britain which is not used to its full potential, simply because people tend to stick to old favourites. My recipes bring together the more traditional Caribbean with my own style to give you some new mouth-watering dishes for the modern palate. West Indian food is a 'rough diamond', but with a little expertise and knowledge we can smooth the edges without ruining its character. Although Caribbean food is a fantastic cuisine in its own right, with influences ranging from Arawak Indian to French and Portuguese, some recipes will reflect its simple basics, but the majority of the recipes are those that have been seen through my eyes – those of the Black Briton who has adapted recipes to suit his palate. I am sure that all the recipes will tantalize and tease your tastebuds, hopefully inspiring you to embrace the food of the Caribbean. It has so much to offer.

When researching the book I was surprised to find out that some of the main Caribbean ingredients – lemons, limes, tamarind, coconuts, sugar cane and plantain – actually came from Spain. The influx of Chinese and East Indians also influenced the way the islanders ate in the past and even now Chinese and Indian descendants still practise old traditions. Now I know why my aunts and uncles like to make the Chinese one-pot meal of fried chicken and egg noodles. A lot of the dishes we eat now are those that were once used to feed the slaves. Saltfish and breadfruit are two examples of cheap provisions which were used. The slaves devised ways of making their food a bit more tasty by using a variety of herbs and spices. The same herbs and spices are an important part of my Caribbean dishes.

Some of these recipes have come from family members who have inspired me over the years and supported me throughout my career, and it is a great pleasure to include them here.

# breakfast

Breakfast is a must. If you ever stay with a Caribbean family, breakfast can turn into a five-course banquet if you're not careful – saying no will only offend, so of course you have to eat it, don't you?

As it's the most important meal of the day, I feel the time should be taken to prepare fresh breakfast food whenever possible, whether it be a bowl of cornmeal porridge or a bowl of fresh fruit. A little bit of time and care will give astounding results.

Breakfast as a child was a wonderful experience, simply because it varied so much. On weekdays it was pretty simple: cereals or the dreaded porridge which made me crawl all the way to school. But Bert (my mother) thought it was central heating for bitter winter mornings.

At Easter and Christmas we would always eat 'festive breakfasts', although they could also be eaten any time of the year. All the family would usually make an effort to get up so that we could eat together. Usually a pretty loud affair, with me being told not to cram so much in my mouth at once. But knowing my uncles, if I didn't get my fill it would all have been eaten by them.

Christmas breakfast could consist of many things, depending on the mood of Bert. From freshly grated cocoa, which would have been a gift from somebody back from their Caribbean travels, to Guinness punch, cerassie tea, fried dumplings, fried ham (cut from ham hocks or from a whole ham), fried plantains, roasted breadfruit, ackee and saltfish, fried fish, fried baked beans, back bacon and eggs cooked in various different ways. Basically, breakfast was one big banquet never to be missed.

# the fruit remedy

Fresh fruit in the morning really perks me up, and I love throwing together a quickie platter.

serves 2

1 pink grapefruit, peeled and segmented
1 ortanique, peeled and segmented
1 jelly coconut, scooped and juiced
2 bananas, peeled and sliced
juice of 1 lime
4 fresh mint leaves, chopped

Once the ingredients are prepared, arrange them on a plate and leave them to sit for 10 minutes before eating. You'll be set for the whole day. Absolutely fabulous!

# the fried remedy

This is my favourite breakfast after a night out on the tiles!

serves 1, if you're feeling greedy
olive oil
2–3 slices of leftover belly pork or ham
1 plantain, peeled and sliced into rounds
1 plum tomato, halved
rock salt and freshly ground black pepper
small knob of butter
2 eggs
½ a 400g/14oz tin of baked beans, fried (optional) (see page 7)
2 slices of fried breadfruit (see page 5)

Heat a little oil in a frying-pan and add the meat slices. Cook until golden brown, then remove from the pan and keep warm. Fry the plantain in the same pan, cooking each side until golden brown, and remove. Keep warm. Season the tomato halves with rock salt and black pepper. Place each half, seed-side down, in the hot pan. Add a small knob of butter and a little more oil and fry until golden brown. Remove the tomatoes from the pan and keep warm.

Wipe the pan clean, add a little more oil and fry the eggs as you like them. Cook the beans, if using.

When everything is ready, simply serve on a plate or use fried breadfruit as a base and serve your Fried Remedy on top of that.

# roast breadfruit

Breadfruit can be found in some supermarkets and at all ethnic food shops or market vegetable stalls. This oval-shaped vegetable is normally about 1kg/2lb 3oz in weight, and is a great substitute for any carbohydrate, such as potatoes. It is normally cooked in its skin, either on the barbecue on a low heat or in a conventional oven at home. It has a beautiful taste when roasted but is also lovely when deep-fried. It can be eaten on its own, or used in stews and salads.

serves 6–8

1 x 1kg/2lb 3oz breadfruit
3 tablespoons olive oil, or 100g/3½oz butter
a pinch of salt
freshly ground black pepper
freshly ground pimento seeds
fresh coriander and parsley, chopped

Preheat the oven to 180°C/350°F/gas 4. Wash the breadfruit and pat dry. Use a fork or a skewer to prick a few holes in the skin. Then wrap the breadfruit in kitchen foil and bake in the preheated oven for 45–60 minutes, turning it every 15 minutes to allow even cooking.

To check if the breadfruit is ready, gently squeeze the outside as you would when baking potatoes. Or unwrap the foil and cut a slice from the breadfruit. It should be soft. When ready, leave to cool. Then peel, slice and either serve as it is or finish off by frying the slices in a pan with the olive oil or butter. Season with salt, black pepper and pimento and serve with the fresh herbs sprinkled on top.

Slices of fried breadfruit are great used as a base for the Fried Remedy (see page 4).

# scrambled eggs

I love scrambled eggs! I cheat when I make them, my secret weapon being the microwave. It gives some of the best results. This simple recipe is delicious! Serve with buttered toast or as an alternative egg dish, in the Fried Remedy (page 4) for instance.

serves 2–3

6 medium eggs
3 tablespoons double cream
2 knobs of butter
a pinch of salt and freshly ground black pepper

Beat the eggs well and mix in the other ingredients. Pour into a bowl and cover with clingfilm. Cook in the microwave for approximately 2 minutes 30 seconds. Check after a minute, stir, and continue cooking – the time in the microwave depends on how runny you like your scrambled eggs. Mix well with a fork before serving, to ruffle the eggs up a bit.

# fried baked beans

You may wonder why I am including this recipe. Although it consists of simply opening a tin of baked beans and warming it up, a few simple additions can give you some excellent variations on this popular breakfast basic. So many ingredients can be added to baked beans to flavour them in different ways: fresh coriander is good, but many other herbs and spices can also be used. Try parsley, thyme, turmeric or curry powder. Bacon works well mixed in with the beans too.

serves 1–2
55g/2oz butter
2 spring onions, finely diced
½ a small red onion, finely diced
1 x 400g/14oz tin of baked beans
freshly ground black pepper

Melt the butter in a pan and cook the spring onions and red onion until soft. Add the beans. Gently simmer until you can smell the flavours of the onions coming through. Season with pepper and serve.

# honey roast ham

This is a great recipe as it provides two meals out of one. For breakfast on Christmas Day we eat most of the roast ham, then the next morning we fry the leftovers and eat it as bacon.

serves 6–8

1 x 4kg/9lb ham, soaked in cold water for 24 hours
4 sticks of celery, washed and halved lengthways
1 leek, washed and halved lengthways
2 onions, roughly chopped
4 carrots, washed and halved lengthways
10 cloves
115g/4oz brown sugar
5 tablespoons honey

for the spice bag

a piece of muslin
a few pimento seeds, crushed
a few white peppercorns, crushed
a few sprigs of fresh thyme
1 bay leaf

Crush the spices and tie them up in the muslin with the herbs. Place the soaked ham in fresh cold water with the spice bag and vegetables. Bring to the boil, skim, and simmer on a low heat for about 3½ hours. Leave to cool in the cooking liquor.

Once the ham has cooled, preheat the oven to 200°C/400°F/gas 6. Remove the rind from the ham, score the fat and stud it with the cloves. Then sprinkle it with the brown sugar, place the ham in a roasting tray and put it into the preheated oven. When the sugar starts to crystallize, pour the honey over the ham and return it to the oven for a further 6–8 minutes. The ham can be served hot or cold. Delicious served with vegetables pickled in chilli vinegar (see page 41).

# fried plantains

Peel 2 plantains and cut them into 4cm/1½ inch pieces. Place in a moderately preheated pan with 2 tablespoons of vegetable oil and fry. The natural sugar in the plantains can caramelize or burn, so keep a close eye on the pan. After 2–3 minutes the plantains should be turned – repeat this until they are all cooked through. They should take about 2 minutes per side.

Remove the plantains from the pan and place on kitchen paper to soak up any excess oil. Sprinkle some chopped fresh coriander over before serving.

# cornmeal porridge

A lovely warming start to the day.

serves 2–4
425ml/¾ pint milk
140ml/¼ pint coconut milk
1 cinnamon stick
140g/5oz cornmeal
1 tablespoon honey or sugar
a pinch of salt
grated nutmeg and ground cinnamon to taste
1 teaspoon vanilla essence

Boil the milk and coconut milk with the cinnamon stick, then add the cornmeal and stir continuously over a moderate heat for 15 minutes. If the porridge is too thick, add a little more milk. Sweeten to taste with the honey or sugar, add a pinch of salt, and finish with nutmeg, cinnamon and vanilla.

# soups

With the soups in this chapter I wanted to combine the old with the new. This is what modern-day eating should be about. Vibrant flavours will stand out, but at the same time be subtle and light. More importantly, these soups are so easy to make.

When I was growing up we didn't really have three-course meals, unless it was Christmas or Easter, simply because of time, but also because the main course was so big there was no room to eat anything else. If you like to have a starter before your main course, then the soups in this chapter are ideal.

# roast plantain soup with fresh ginger chantilly

This is a very quick and easy soup to prepare; full of flavour, using one of the most popular and versatile vegetables in the Caribbean.

serves 4

2 ripe plantains
4 tablespoons olive oil
1 red chilli, finely chopped
2 cloves of garlic, crushed
1 large red onion, finely chopped
1 leek, roughly chopped
1 beef tomato, roughly chopped
3 teaspoons chopped fresh ginger
2 sprigs of fresh thyme, leaves picked
salt and freshly ground black pepper
1.7 litres/3 pints chicken or vegetable stock
2 tablespoons chopped fresh coriander

for the chantilly

140ml/¼ pint double cream
1 teaspoon chopped pickled ginger

Peel the plantain and chop roughly.

Preheat the oven to 200°C/400°F/gas 6. Warm 2 tablespoons of the olive oil in a roasting tray, add the plantain and roast in the preheated oven for approximately 5–8 minutes.

Place all the other vegetables and herbs in a large pan with the rest of the oil and soften over a moderate heat. Add the roasted plantain to the other vegetables, lightly season and add the stock. Leave to simmer for approximately 15 minutes.

Liquidize the soup in a food processor and correct the seasoning.

To make the chantilly, whip the cream to soft peaks and add the pickled ginger, then season with salt and pepper.

Serve the soup with a dollop of the ginger chantilly and a sprinkling of chopped coriander.

# oxtail soup

This soup is definitely all about flavours. The Caribbean is renowned for its hot food, and in some cases that reputation holds true. This recipe, however, shows the balance and subtlety in flavours which can also be found throughout the Caribbean.

My mother would usually serve this as two separate dishes: first the soup liquid on its own, and then the meat and dumplings. I prefer it as one complete meal but you can serve it either way.

serves 4

2 oxtails, cut up
olive oil
115g/4oz flour (optional)
1 tablespoon tomato purée
beef stock or water, to cover
boiled dumplings (see page 37)
2 onions, finely chopped
4 spring onions, chopped
1 Scotch bonnet chilli
3 cloves of garlic, crushed
225g/8oz smoked streaky bacon, cut into large lardons
6 pimento seeds, crushed
salt and freshly ground black pepper
1 christophene, diced
2 potatoes, peeled and diced
a small handful of fresh parsley, chopped

for the marinade

1 x 75cl bottle of red wine
1 bulb of garlic, halved crossways
2 large carrots, chopped roughly
1 large bunch of fresh thyme
6 pimento seeds, crushed
2 bay leaves

First wash the oxtails thoroughly, then dry them and put them into a large bowl with all the marinade ingredients. This should be done 12–24 hours before the soup is made, to give a really piquant flavour to the meat, complementing the natural sweet oxtail flavour.

Remove the oxtails from the marinade and dry on a tea-towel. Heat some olive oil in a large saucepan and brown the oxtails evenly on all sides. (Optional: the oxtails can be dipped in flour before frying to improve the colour and consistency of the soup.) Remove the oxtails from the pan and add the vegetables from the marinade. Fry on a high heat until well browned, then add the tomato purée and any remaining marinade liquor and simmer to reduce. Return the oxtails to the pan, cover with beef stock or water, and cook over a gentle heat for approximately 1½ hours, or until the meat is tender.

While the oxtails are cooking, make your dumplings (see page 37).

Once the meat is cooked, remove the oxtails and all the vegetables from the pan. Discard the vegetables, retaining the meat and cooking liquor. In another pan soften the onions, spring onions, Scotch bonnet, garlic, bacon and pimento and season with salt and pepper (not too much salt, as the bacon is already salty). Add the reserved cooking liquor and bring to the boil. Now add the christophene, potatoes and dumplings and leave to cook for 6–8 minutes. Return the oxtails to the pan and continue cooking for another 2 minutes. Add the parsley and serve.

# pig trotter soup

4 pig's trotters
3.4 litres/6 pints water
4 cloves of garlic
1 bay leaf
1 small bunch of fresh thyme
6 black peppercorns
6 pimento seeds
2 medium onions, 1 roughly chopped, 1 diced
2 carrots, 1 roughly chopped, 1 diced
4 sticks of celery, 2 roughly chopped, 2 diced
olive oil
2 tablespoons chopped flat-leaf parsley

Rinse the trotters well in cold water. Roughly chop them and put them in a large saucepan. Cover with the water and add the garlic, bay leaf, thyme, peppercorns, pimento seeds and the roughly chopped vegetables. Cook for 2 hours, making sure you keep the trotters submerged in the cooking liquid. Add more water as necessary. The meat is ready when it comes away from the bone. Remove the meat and the vegetables from the liquid. Reserve the liquid.

Cook the diced vegetables in olive oil until soft. Pour on the reserved liquid and simmer for a further 10 minutes. Shred the trotter meat and add to soup. Finish this flavoursome broth with some chopped flat-leaf parsley.

# pepperpot soup

Pepperpot soup is one of the most popular dishes of the Caribbean, and is cooked in different ways throughout the region. In days of old, meat was the principal part of the dish, which was preserved in cassareep, the poisonous juice of the cassava. Here is my own version of this classic dish. You will need to marinate the beef for at least 2 hours before starting to cook.

serves 4

455g/1lb stewing beef, cut into 2.5cm/1 inch pieces
salt and freshly ground black and white pepper
6 pimento seeds, crushed
3 Scotch bonnet chillies
4 tablespoons olive oil
1 onion, chopped
2 cloves of garlic, crushed
2 sprigs of fresh thyme
1.8 litres/3 pints water
1.8 litres/3 pints beef stock
285ml/½ pint coconut milk
2–3 bay leaves
1 large carrot, diced
1 potato, diced
1 red pepper, diced
1 christophene, diced
a handful of spinach or callaloo

Season the beef well with black and white pepper and crushed pimento seeds. Crush 2 of the Scotch bonnet chillies and rub into the meat. Leave to marinate for 2–4 hours or as long as possible.

When you are ready to make the soup, heat the olive oil in a thick-bottomed pan and brown the meat well on all sides. Remove from the pan. Add the onion, garlic, thyme and remaining Scotch bonnet chilli to the pan and cook gently for 2–3 minutes. Put the meat back into the pan and add the water, stock, coconut milk and bay leaves.

Simmer the soup gently for 45–60 minutes or until the beef is tender. Add the carrot, potato, red pepper and christophene and cook for a further 5 minutes. Season. Just before serving, stir in the spinach or callaloo leaves.

# butter bean soup

serves 4–6

½ an onion, diced
1 chilli, diced
2 sticks of celery, diced
1 leek, diced
2 cloves of garlic
olive oil
salt and freshly ground black pepper
225g/8oz dried butter beans, soaked overnight
2–3 sprigs of fresh thyme
1 bay leaf
3 pimento seeds
1.4 litres/2½ pints chicken or vegetable stock

Put all the vegetables in a large pan with some olive oil, salt and pepper and cook over a medium heat until soft. Add the soaked butter beans and cook for a little while longer, adding the thyme, bay leaf and pimento seeds, which will give off a lovely fragrance.

Add the stock and cook for about 30–45 minutes until the beans are soft. Liquidize in a food processor or blender, check the seasoning and serve.

# salads

I really can't remember eating much salad as a child.
At that age I was quite happy not to, but now that I've
learnt about all the different leaves and salad
ingredients my attitude towards salads has changed.
Now I love to eat them.

   With the wealth of imported and home-grown
produce now available in Britain, there is no reason for
us to eat plain old boring salads. I hope these recipes
will inspire you to create a few fantastic ones yourself –
let that culinary beast free, go on!

# jerk chicken with watercress and cashew nut dressing

This makes a beautiful starter or main course. It is a very simple, but vibrant and mouth-watering combination. The chicken needs to be marinated for at least 2 hours. It can be cooked on a griddle plate or under a grill, but the taste of charcoal from a barbecue will really bring the dish alive.

serves 4 as a starter, 2 as a main

8 chicken thighs
1 x jerk seasoning (see page 177, or from a bottle)
55g/2oz cashew nuts
1 tablespoon honey
3 dessertspoons sherry vinegar
3 dessertspoons arachide oil or groundnut oil
salt and freshly ground black pepper
115g/4oz christophene
1 large bunch of watercress

Put the chicken thighs into the jerk seasoning and leave to marinate for at least 2 hours before you want to cook. Then remove them from the marinade and grill on a hot barbecue, turning them frequently. When coloured on both sides, move them to the side of the griddle to continue cooking slowly.

Toast the cashew nuts under a medium-hot grill – this takes no time at all, so keep an eye on them or they will end up burnt! Leave them to one side to cool.

Now make your dressing by whisking the honey, vinegar and oil together in a bowl. Add some salt and pepper. Finely slice the christophene and cut into long strips. Put into a salad bowl with the watercress and pour the dressing over. Cut the chicken into thick strips and place on top of the salad. Sprinkle with the toasted cashews and serve.

# chicken and guacamole salad

The chicken needs to be marinated for 24 hours.

serves 2
2 boneless chicken breasts
1 little gem or cos lettuce

for the marinade
1 clove of garlic, crushed
1 chilli, finely chopped
½ a bunch of fresh coriander, chopped
salt and freshly ground black pepper
4 tablespoons olive oil

for the guacamole
3 avocados, peeled, deseeded and diced
1 red onion, finely diced
1 chilli, finely diced
2 plum tomatoes, peeled, deseeded and diced
zest and juice of 1 lime
½ a bunch of fresh coriander, chopped
salt and freshly ground black pepper

Put the chicken breasts into a bowl, add the marinade ingredients, and leave in the refrigerator for 24 hours.

Preheat the oven to 180°C/350°F/gas 4. Heat a griddle pan and brown the chicken on all sides, then transfer to the oven for approximately 6–8 minutes. Remove from the oven and leave to rest in a warm place.

Meanwhile, mix together all the guacamole ingredients. Season to taste. Slice the chicken and serve with the lettuce and a good dollop of guacamole.

# marinated chicken salad with paw-paw salsa and deep-fried filo pastry

This salad, accompanied by a glass or two of ice-cold rum punch, is perfect for a summer's day.

serves 4

olive oil
4 boneless chicken breasts
115ml/4fl oz coconut oil
chicken stock
2 sheets of filo pastry

for the marinade

½ a bunch of fresh coriander, chopped
4 chillies, halved and deseeded
2 tablespoons curry powder
1 tablespoon chopped garlic
1 red onion, roughly sliced
zest of 1 lime
1 stick of cinnamon

for the paw-paw salsa

2 paw-paws, finely diced
1 tablespoon honey
1 chilli, finely diced
salt and pepper
zest and juice of 1 lime
2 tablespoons olive oil
2 tablespoons chopped fresh coriander

Heat a little olive oil in a pan and add all the marinade ingredients. Cook gently until the onion is softened. Put the chicken breasts into a bowl, and add the marinade ingredients and the coconut oil. Top up with olive oil to cover the chicken. Leave for 4–6 hours.

Remove the chicken from the marinade, drain off any excess oil, and roll the chicken in clingfilm and then in kitchen foil. Poach in chicken stock for 6–8 minutes, then leave to cool.

Heat a little olive oil in a frying pan. Unwrap the chicken, season with salt and pepper, and gently fry on both sides until lightly browned.

Mix all the salsa ingredients together.

Cut out 12 rounds of filo with a medium-size pastry cutter, using 2 sheets at a time. Deep-fry in moderately hot oil for 30–45 seconds. Remove the pastry from the fryer and lay on kitchen paper to drain. Lightly season with salt and pepper and a sprinkling of curry powder. (These are really fab!)

To serve the salad, slice the chicken, lay some on one round of filo pastry, followed by some salsa, place another round of filo on top and repeat the layers. Top with a final round of filo and scatter the rest of the salsa around the dish.

# confit duck salad

serves 2

2 confit duck legs, shredded (see page 97)
2 spring onions, cut in julienne strips
½ a Scotch bonnet chilli, finely diced
a handful of beansprouts
½ a cucumber, cut in julienne strips
2 tomatoes, cut in strips
salt and freshly ground black pepper
a good handful of curly endive

for the dressing
1 shallot, finely diced
½ tablespoon finely diced garlic
juice of 1 lime
juice of 1 orange
4–5 tablespoons tomato ketchup
1 tablespoon honey

Confit the duck legs (see page 97) and shred while still warm.

Mix all the vegetables in a bowl and season lightly. Mix the endive with the vegetables and sprinkle with a little salt. Mix together all the dressing ingredients. Arrange the salad on a serving dish and top with the confit duck. Drizzle a little dressing over before serving.

see page 4

the fried remedy

see pages 5, 12  left roast breadfruit; right roast plantain soup with fresh ginger chantilly

see page 46 citrus oyster treats

see page 20

jerk chicken with watercress and cashew
nut dressing

see page 27 | crab and mango salad

see pages
31, 29, 22–3

top left roast beetroot with chilli and red onion salad; top right salad of sweet potato and asparagus; bottom left marinated chicken salad with paw-paw salsa and deep-fried filo pastry

see page 36 | johnny cakes

see page 38 patties

# fiery oyster salad

serves 2
6 oysters
4 rashers of smoked streaky bacon, cut into lardons
2 Scotch bonnet chillies, finely diced
1 small red onion, finely diced
mixed salad leaves
10 sprigs of fresh coriander

for the dressing
85ml/3fl oz groundnut oil
85ml/3fl oz olive oil
55ml/2fl oz balsamic vinegar

Prepare the oysters as for the Citrus Oyster Treats on page 46, reserving any juice but discarding the shells.

Fry the bacon until crisp, remove from the pan and cool. Add the Scotch bonnets and red onion to the pan and quickly stir-fry, being careful not to colour the vegetables, then leave to one side to cool.

Meanwhile, carefully pick and wash the salad leaves, adding a few whole leaves of coriander to the salad to give a really tangy citrus flavour.

Add a little of the dressing and oyster juice to the peppers and red onion. Spread this all over a serving plate, arrange the oysters on top, then sprinkle with the crispy lardons and top it all with salad leaves. Garnish with chopped coriander and serve with the rest of the dressing.

# crab and avocado salad

This recipe is best made with pre-picked white crabmeat, rather than picking the flesh yourself from fresh hen crabs, because the yield will vary and you could be there all day instead of enjoying yourself. Picked crabmeat is available in most supermarkets.

serves 4

400g/14oz white crabmeat
juice of 1 lime
2–3 tablespoons mayonnaise
salt and freshly ground black pepper
cayenne pepper, to taste
3 avocados, peeled, deseeded and diced
1 tomato, peeled, deseeded and diced
1 Scotch bonnet chilli, deseeded and finely diced
3 tablespoons chopped fresh coriander
2 good handfuls of mixed salad leaves
2 tablespoons curry oil (see page 190)

Mix the crabmeat with the lime juice and mayonnaise. Season well with salt, pepper and cayenne and refrigerate.

Mix the avocados with the tomato, chilli and coriander, being careful not to break the avocados up too much.

Spoon the avocado mix into a ring, top with the crabmeat, garnish with the salad leaves and finish with a drizzle of curry oil.

# crab and mango salad

I would suggest using picked white crabmeat for this recipe, as for the previous salad.

serves 4
400g/14oz white crabmeat
juice of 1 lime
2–3 tablespoons mayonnaise
3 mangoes, peeled, deseeded and diced
fresh coriander leaves

for the dressing
3 tablespoons coconut water
2 tablespoons lime juice
1 tablespoon pimento oil (see page 189)
1 red chilli
3 tablespoons freshly grated coconut
1 tablespoon olive oil
a splash of lime juice
salt and freshly ground black pepper

Mix the crabmeat with the lime juice and mayonnaise and refrigerate.
   Combine the dressing ingredients. Add the mangoes. Spoon half the mangoes into a ring and top with the white crabmeat. Top with the rest of the mangoes. Garnish with coriander leaves.

# sweet potato salad

This salad can be made using either mayonnaise or vinaigrette – both ways work well.

serves 4

4 orange-fleshed sweet potatoes
salt and freshly ground black pepper
3 tablespoons mayonnaise or vinaigrette
2 spring onions, finely chopped
1 small bunch of chives, finely chopped
2 tablespoons chopped flat-leaf parsley
a pinch of cayenne

Peel the sweet potatoes and cut into 1cm/½ inch dice. Boil for approximately 10–15 minutes, making sure you don't overcook them. Leave them to cool naturally, and season lightly.

If using mayonnaise, place it in a bowl – if you feel it's too thick, add 1 tablespoon of water to thin it down. Add the spring onions and chives and pour over the cooled sweet potatoes. Gently turn the mixture without breaking the potatoes up. Check the seasoning and sprinkle with chopped parsley and a pinch of cayenne. Chill and serve.

If using vinaigrette, pour it over the potatoes while they are still warm. When cool, add all other ingredients, omitting the mayonnaise.

# salad of sweet potato and asparagus

This dish is one of my favourite salads – I love making it. It makes a great starter or main course.

serves 4

795g/1¾lb sweet potatoes, peeled and sliced
salt and freshly ground black pepper
2 tablespoons balsamic vinegar
4 tablespoons white wine vinegar
8 tablespoons olive oil
½ a red onion
16 asparagus spears
4 large eggs
2 good handfuls of mixed salad leaves

Cook the sweet potatoes in salted water for approximately 8–10 minutes, or until tender. While still warm, dress with half the balsamic and white wine vinegar and half the olive oil. The potatoes will soak up the flavour as they cool. Finely dice the red onion and sprinkle over the potatoes.

Trim and peel the asparagus spears. Plunge into boiling salted water, and cook for 3–4 minutes. Drain and place in ice-cold water to refresh. Once the spears are cool, remove them from the water or they will lose their delicate flavour.

Boil the eggs for approximately 4–5 minutes. Cool, shell, and cut into quarters.

Mix the remaining vinegar and oil to make the dressing. Arrange the mixed leaves on a serving plate, put the salad ingredients on top and pour over the dressing.

# roast pumpkin and apricot salad with a cumin and pimento dressing

serves 4

1 small pumpkin, peeled and diced
4 apricots, quartered and stoned
rocket leaves, to garnish
2 tablespoons chopped fresh coriander
2 tablespoons chopped fresh parsley

for the dressing

½ tablespoon cumin seeds
½ tablespoon ground pimento seeds
4 tablespoons olive oil
1 finely diced shallot
2 tablespoons sherry vinegar

To make the dressing, preheat the oven to 180°C/350°F/gas 4. Place the cumin seeds in an ovenproof frying-pan and put into the oven. Toast for about 3–4 minutes, or until you start to get a strong fragrant smell. Add the pimento and a little oil to the frying-pan, add the shallots and cook until they are soft. Add the olive oil and sherry vinegar, transfer to a bowl, and leave to cool.

Using the frying-pan the spices were cooked in, add more oil and cook the pumpkin. This should take about 5–8 minutes – don't overcook it; make sure the pumpkin is still firm. Leave to cool. Mix the apricots with the pumpkin, rocket leaves and herbs, and pour over the cumin and allspice dressing.

# roast beetroot with chilli and red onion salad

A really wonderful, lively salad, full of flavour and, of course, combining some vibrant colours. Enjoy.

serves 2

3 medium beetroots
2 cloves
2 cinnamon sticks
3 tablespoons olive oil
½ teaspoon finely chopped garlic
1 small bunch of fresh thyme, leaves picked
2 spring onions, finely diced
1 Scotch bonnet chilli, finely diced
1 red onion, sliced into rings
2 tablespoons balsamic vinegar
salt and freshly ground black pepper
a good handful of mixed salad leaves

Preheat the oven to 180°C/350°F/gas 4.

Parboil the beetroot for 15 minutes in boiling, salted water, with the cloves and cinnamon sticks – both spices are fabulous with beetroot. Remove from the heat and when cool, peel and quarter the beetroot. Place in a preheated roasting tray, with the olive oil, garlic and thyme.

Cook in the oven for 10 minutes or until the beetroot are soft. Leave to cool. Combine with the other ingredients, and serve.

# tomato and onion salad

serves 4

4 plum tomatoes
2 beef tomatoes
8 cherry tomatoes
rock salt and freshly ground black pepper
6 tablespoons olive oil
1 red onion
a small handful of fresh basil, leaves picked

Pour boiling water over the plum tomatoes and leave for approximately 10 seconds. When their skins start to break, plunge them into ice-cold water for 15–20 seconds and then remove the skins and slice.

Slice the beef tomatoes into 4 or 5 pieces and halve the cherry tomatoes. Arrange all the tomatoes on a serving plate. Sprinkle with rock salt, black pepper and a good drizzle of olive oil.

Slice the red onion and shred the basil leaves, and sprinkle both over the salad.

# caribbean coleslaw

This is a gorgeous but simple salad which has loads of texture. Raw Savoy cabbage is just beautiful in any salad.

serves 4

3 medium carrots, thinly sliced
½ a christophene, thinly sliced
½ a small white onion, thinly sliced
1 Savoy cabbage, shredded
salt and freshly ground black pepper
3–4 tablespoons mayonnaise
3 tablespoons chopped fresh coriander
a little sugar (optional)

Prepare and combine all the vegetables. Add seasoning and stir in the mayonnaise. Finish off with chopped coriander and a sprinkling of sugar if you want. Chill and serve.

This coleslaw will keep in the fridge for 3 days.

# christophene and carrot remoulade

This goes really well with all sorts of cold meats or with barbecued meat.

serves 2

2 christophenes, thinly sliced
1 large carrot, thinly sliced
1 spring onion, finely diced
1 tablespoon grain or Dijon mustard
3–4 tablespoons mayonnaise

Mix the vegetables together, then stir in the mustard and mayonnaise. Chill and serve.

# snacks

Some of the snacks in this chapter are typically
Caribbean, like my favourite patties and coconut
drops. Try making these – you will not be disappointed.
Others included here may surprise you: the macaroni
cheese, for example. Caribbeans love this dish – I hope
you like my version. Sometimes a snack can be a light
evening meal, at other times simply a nibble between
meals. Either way, I hope you find these combinations
delicious!

# johnny cakes

These cakes are an absolute legend – they can be eaten with anything, as part of a Caribbean breakfast, as well as on their own.

makes 6–8

1 teaspoon sugar
a pinch of salt
200g/7oz self-raising flour
50g/1¾oz margarine
125ml/4½fl oz water
4 tablespoons coconut oil

Sift the sugar, salt and flour into a bowl. Rub in the margarine, then make a well in the centre. Gradually mix in the water to make a soft dough. Divide this into little balls and knead each for 30 seconds to 1 minute.

Fry the cakes in the coconut oil on a moderate heat until they are golden brown on each side.

# boiled dumplings

Dumplings are the pasta of the Caribbean. They can be served with most main courses. For such a simple dish these delicacies are absolutely gorgeous.

makes 5–6 dumplings

**175g/6oz plain flour**
**a pinch of salt**
**75ml/3fl oz water**

Bring a pan of salted water to the boil. Put the flour in a bowl with the salt. Add the measured water gradually, stirring continually until you have a dough, and knead into a ball. Shape into little balls or sausage shapes and gently simmer them in the water for about 10 minutes.

# patties

These patties can be filled with minced lamb, chicken, vegetables or saltfish and ackee and are ideal served with a variety of side dishes. Seasoned rice (see page 115) is a real favourite of mine.

makes 6 large or 14 small patties

for the filling

3 tablespoons vegetable oil
455g/1lb of your chosen meat or fish, minced
1 small onion, finely diced
½ a red pepper, finely diced
1 Scotch bonnet chilli, finely diced
1 clove of garlic, crushed
2 teaspoons Madras curry powder
1 teaspoon turmeric or saffron
1 teaspoon garam masala
3 pimento seeds, ground
a pinch of ground cinnamon
a pinch of ground ginger
salt and freshly ground black pepper
1 dessertspoon tomato purée
285ml/½ pint stock

Heat the oil in a thick-bottomed pan. Add your chosen meat or fish and fry till brown all over. Remove from the pan and drain off the fat. Add all the vegetables to the pan and cook for a couple of minutes. Then add all the spices and cook for a further 3 minutes. Put the meat or fish back into the pan with the vegetables, add the tomato purée, followed by the stock, and continue to cook until the liquid has reduced. Remove from the heat and leave to cool until you're ready to make the patties.

The best pastry to use for making patties is puff pastry. Simply buy a packet of ready-made from the supermarket.

200g/7oz puff pastry
1 teaspoon turmeric
1 teaspoon curry powder
a pinch of ground cumin
a pinch of cayenne

Dry roast the spices in a moderate oven for 2–3 minutes, being careful not to let them burn. Leave to cool, then fold into the pastry. Roll the pastry out to about 0.5cm/¼ inch thick, then cut out either 14 x 12cm/ 5 inch discs or 6 x 20cm/8 inch discs. Place a little filling on one side of each disc and brush the edges of the disc with water.

Fold over and seal together, pinching the edge between your thumb and forefinger to seal the patty. Or use a fork to push down on the edge. Place in the refrigerator for 20 minutes before cooking. Preheat the oven to 190°C/375°F/gas 5.

Place the patties on a lightly greased baking sheet. Perforate the tops and cook for approximately 15–20 minutes or until golden.

# macaroni cheese

I have no idea why Caribbeans like macaroni cheese so much. At most family gatherings or functions someone will bring along their version of this popular dish. This is mine – I hope you enjoy it.

serves 4

140g/5oz macaroni
olive oil
salt and freshly ground black pepper
1 teaspoon Dijon mustard
1 egg yolk (optional)
a pinch of cayenne
a pinch of grated nutmeg
850ml/1½ pints Mornay sauce (see page 163)
140g/5oz grated Cheddar or Gruyère cheese

Preheat the oven to 180°C/350°F/gas 4. Bring a large pan of salted water to the boil and add the macaroni with a good lug of olive oil. Let the water come back to the boil and cook for 10–15 minutes, stirring occasionally. Drain the pasta, season, and stir in a little more olive oil. Put the pasta into a bowl and mix in the Dijon mustard and egg yolk (if using). Season with salt, pepper, cayenne and nutmeg. Place in an ovenproof dish, pour the Mornay sauce over, and sprinkle with the grated cheese. Cook in the preheated oven for 10 minutes or until the cheese is golden brown.

# pickled vegetables

These go great with cold meats.

3 onions, sliced into rings
4 cloves of garlic, peeled and sliced
2 red peppers, cut into batons
3 carrots, sliced
white wine vinegar, enough to cover the vegetables
1 whole chilli
4 sprigs of fresh thyme
10 black peppercorn seeds, crushed
10 pimento seeds, coarsely crushed

Blanch the onions, garlic, peppers and carrots in salted boiling water for 2 minutes and drain. Then place in a fresh pan, add the white wine vinegar, chilli, thyme, peppercorns and pimento seeds and bring back to the boil. Leave in the liquid until cold. Put into an airtight jar and refrigerate until ready to use. These pickled vegetables will keep in the fridge for about a month.

# spiced short pastry

This pastry is best made 2 hours before use. It's a beautiful recipe for making a quick base and it's especially good when used as a savoury tartlet shell. See the next two recipes for suggested tartlet fillings.

1 teaspoon turmeric
1 teaspoon curry powder
a pinch of ground cumin
a pinch of cayenne
a pinch of salt
200g/7oz plain flour
100g/3½oz good-quality butter, very cold
2 tablespoons ice cold water

Dry roast the spices on a tray in a moderate oven for 2–3 minutes, being careful not to burn them. Remove from the tray and leave to cool.

Sift the salt and flour into a bowl and mix in the spices. Add the butter and rub together until the mixture resembles a crumble. Add the water gradually until you have a workable dough.

Dust the work surface with flour, turn the dough out on to the surface and shape into a rectangle, gently rolling and keeping that rectangular shape at all times! Wrap in clingfilm and refrigerate for 2 hours.

# ackee and saltfish tartlets

This tartlet recipe comes in quite handy for using up any leftovers you may have in the fridge. It can be served with a salad as a light evening meal.

makes 6 tartlets
1 x spiced short pastry recipe (page 42)
3 handfuls of dried beans

for the egg mix
4 eggs
285ml/½ pint cream
285ml/½ pint milk
salt and freshly ground black pepper

for the filling
450g/1lb salt cod, freshly salted if possible, poached lightly in a little milk
  then flaked
200g/7oz tinned ackee, chopped
1 spring onion, chopped
1 tomato, peeled, deseeded and chopped
½ Scotch bonnet chilli, chopped
1 clove of garlic, chopped
2 tablespoons olive oil
1 tablespoon tomato fondue (see page 167)

Preheat the oven to 190°C/375°F/gas 5.

Beat the eggs well. Add the cream and milk and mix together. Season.

Mix all the filling ingredients together in a separate bowl.

Line 6 x 12–15cm/5–6 inch round pastry tins with short pastry, cover completely with greaseproof paper, add the beans and bake blind for 5–8 minutes. Once the pastry is firm, take out of the oven, remove the beans and greaseproof paper and sprinkle a little ackee and saltfish filling in each tartlet case. Reduce the oven temperature to 170°C/325°F/gas 3.

Add the egg mix to each tartlet and gently bake for 10–15 minutes, making sure the eggs are cooked until firm enough to serve hot or cold. Either way makes a beautiful snack.

# callaloo and poached egg tartlets

makes 4 tartlets

1 x spiced short pastry recipe (page 42)
3 good handfuls of dried beans
1 onion, finely diced
1 clove of garlic, finely diced
olive oil
a pinch of freshly ground pimento seeds
1 x 400g/14oz tin of callaloo or 1kg/2lb 3oz freshly picked spinach
8 eggs
3 tablespoons white wine vinegar

Preheat the oven to 190°C/375°F/gas 5. Line 4 x 12–15cm/5–6 inch round pastry tins with short pastry, cover completely with greaseproof paper, and bake them blind with the beans for 5–8 minutes. Remove beans and greaseproof paper and return to the oven for a further 5 minutes, or until golden brown. Meanwhile, cook the onions and garlic in a little olive oil. Add the pimento, then the callaloo or spinach, and continue cooking for 2 minutes.

Poach the eggs in water with the white wine vinegar for approximately 4–8 minutes, depending on how set you like them. Place some callaloo in the bottom of each tart shell and top each with 2 poached eggs. Serve hot.

# citrus oyster treats

One of the most talked about fruits of the sea is the oyster, and whether you love them or hate them, they are certainly the heroes of the shellfish world. In Britain, when the native oyster is in season, it is, in my opinion, the best in the world. When they are not available, rock or Pacific oysters are good to cook with, although the native British ones are much better for eating raw because of their wonderful flavour.

These treats are the culinary equivalent of salt and vinegar crisps, believe it or not. The natural saltiness of the oysters is offset by the tangy citrus flavours – lovely.

serves 2

6 oysters, with their juice
2 shallots, finely diced
red wine to cover the shallots
3 pink grapefruits
3 oranges
10 fresh lemon balm leaves, shredded

To open the oysters, insert an oyster knife firmly into the hinges of each shell and twist. The shell will become loose and you will be able to open it up. Discard the top part of the shell and loosen the oyster from the main part by cutting it away. Put the oysters with their juice into a bowl and refrigerate. Wash the shells and set aside.

Simmer the shallots over a low heat in enough red wine to cover them. While they are cooking, peel the grapefruits and oranges and segment them (reserving the juice), then mix the lemon balm through the segments. Add the oyster and fruit juices. Mix the shallots with the fruit.

To serve, place a spoonful of fruit mixture into the bottom of each shell and place an oyster on top.

# vegetables

Vegetables are a very important part of the Caribbean
diet. With many Caribbean dishes being of the one-pot
variety, you always seem to get vegetables whether
you like it or not – and of course you have to eat them.
My favourite vegetable is plantain, a member of the
banana family, and I have included it in a few recipes,
as well as callaloo, a very versatile green leafy
vegetable.

# okra, christophene and plantain casserole

A really nice accompaniment to fried fish.

serves 4–6

3 tablespoons coconut oil
1 tablespoon coriander seeds, freshly ground
1 tablespoon cumin seeds, freshly ground
a pinch of saffron strands
4 spring onions, chopped
2 cloves of garlic, finely chopped
3 christophenes, peeled and quartered
200g/7oz okra, topped and tailed
6 beef tomatoes, peeled, deseeded and chopped
2 plantains, peeled and diced
salt and freshly ground black pepper
3 tablespoons chopped fresh coriander

Heat the coconut oil in a pan and lightly cook the ground coriander and cumin, saffron, spring onions and garlic. Add the christophenes and cook for a further 2–3 minutes, then remove from the pan.

Add the okra and chopped tomatoes to the pan and simmer covered for 5–8 minutes. Add the plantains and the christophenes and cook until tender. Season, and sprinkle with chopped coriander.

# butternut squash and vegetable curry

This is a fantastic vegetarian dish. Simple but very impressive – it can even tempt a carnivore like me.

serves 4–6

5 tablespoons olive oil
2 red onions, peeled and diced
4 cloves, crushed
1 tablespoon roasted cumin seeds
1 small bunch of fresh thyme
3 cloves of garlic, finely chopped
1 aubergine, diced
1 red pepper, diced
1 yellow pepper, diced
2 christophenes, peeled and diced
2 baby butternut or spaghetti squash, halved and diced
6 tomatoes, diced
chopped fresh parsley, to garnish

Warm the oil in a thick-bottomed pan, add the onions, cloves, cumin, thyme and garlic and cook until the vegetables are translucent. Remove from the pan and set aside. Add the aubergine to the pan and cook until browned. Remove from the pan. Add the peppers, christophene and squash to the pan and cook for 2–3 minutes. Return the aubergines and onions to the pan with the tomatoes and continue cooking for 5–10 minutes.

Serve sprinkled with parsley. This goes well with seasoned or tomato rice (see pages 115 and 116).

# butternut squash dauphinoise

serves 4–6

2 butternut squash, peeled and diced
140ml/¼ pint milk
565ml/1 pint double cream
6 cloves of garlic, crushed or finely chopped
salt and freshly ground black pepper
1 tablespoon ground cinnamon
1 tablespoon freshly grated nutmeg

Preheat the oven to 180°C/350°F/gas 4. Slice the squash lengthways into strips approximately 0.5cm/¼ inch thick.

Put the milk, cream and garlic into a pan, season lightly and bring to the boil. Arrange the squash in layers in an ovenware dish, ladling the cream mixture over each layer of squash and dusting each layer with cinnamon and nutmeg, salt and pepper. Cover the dish with greaseproof paper and bake in the preheated oven for 15–20 minutes. Check whether the squash is cooked by piercing it with the tip of a sharp knife.

# roast potatoes

I find the best way to cook roast potatoes is to use this recipe, which gives you the best of both worlds: really crispy on the outside and soft and fluffy on the inside. This method can also be used with other vegetables such as sweet potatoes.

serves 4

4 large red-skinned potatoes, peeled and cut in large dice
salt and freshly ground black pepper
4 tablespoons oil
1 tablespoon fresh thyme leaves
4 cloves of garlic, chopped
90g/3½oz butter
a small handful of fresh parsley, chopped

Preheat the oven to 220°C/425°F/gas 7.

Put the potatoes into a pan of salted water and bring to the boil. Simmer for 2–3 minutes, then drain in a colander.

Reheat the pan and add the oil. Add the potatoes, thyme and garlic and cook until golden brown. Place on a baking tray in the preheated oven and cook for approximately 15–20 minutes, adding some of the butter to the tray every 5 minutes.

When the potatoes are cooked, lay them on kitchen paper to drain. Sprinkle with chopped parsley and serve.

# sautéed sweet potatoes

serves 4

2 large orange-fleshed sweet potatoes
4 tablespoons olive oil
salt and freshly ground black pepper
cayenne
70g/2½oz butter
2 teaspoons chopped fresh parsley
2 teaspoons chopped fresh chives

Place the scrubbed sweet potatoes in cold water, bring to the boil, and parboil for 5–8 minutes. Drain and leave to cool. When cool enough to handle, carefully remove the skins, being careful not to cut too deep, and slice the potatoes into 1cm/½ inch slices. Heat the oil in a pan and fry the potatoes until coloured on both sides.

Season with salt, pepper and cayenne, then add the butter and leave on the heat until it starts to froth and brown – this will make the potatoes really buttery and crispy. Sprinkle with chopped parsley and chives, and serve.

# christophene and sweet potato

I recommend that you try this dish, the Caribbean version of potato gratin.

serves 4–6

850ml/1½ pints double cream
6 cloves of garlic, finely chopped
butter
2 christophenes, peeled and thinly sliced
2 sweet potatoes, peeled and thinly sliced
salt and freshly ground black pepper
140g/5oz grated cheese (optional)

Preheat the oven to 180°C/350°F/gas 4. Finely chop half the garlic. Gently heat the cream with the chopped garlic and leave to infuse. Butter the dish in which the potatoes will be cooked and rub the inside of the dish with the rest of the garlic cloves, cut in half. Arrange alternate layers of christophene and sweet potato in the dish, coating each layer with cream and seasoning with salt and pepper (if cheese is being used, sprinkle it over each layer). When you reach the top of the dish, pour one last ladle of cream over and place in the preheated oven for 30–45 minutes. When cooked, the top layer should be a lovely golden brown.

# garlic mashed potato

This is one of my favourite recipes simply because of the amazing flavour and texture of the finished dish. I recommend eating it with red snapper.

905g/2lb potatoes, peeled and diced
6 cloves of garlic
160g/6oz unsalted butter
155ml/5½fl oz milk or double cream
salt and white pepper

Place the potatoes in a large pan and just cover with water. Boil for 15–20 minutes. While the potatoes are cooking, take a smaller pan and boil some water. Add the whole garlic cloves for a couple of minutes and then remove them. Blanch them like this in fresh water a further five or six times. When the garlic has cooled, crush and purée the cloves until smooth. Drain the potatoes when they are cooked and leave them to dry out, then purée them by putting them through a mouli or potato ricer, adding the butter at the same time. This will give you very smooth mashed potato. Bring the milk or cream to the boil and add to the mash. Beat well, season, and add the garlic purée to taste.

# plantain mash

This versatile vegetable is beautiful and sweet and a perfect accompaniment to any fish or meat dish. A lovely alternative to mashed potato.

serves 2

2 ripe plantains
85ml/3fl oz olive oil
1 teaspoon fresh thyme leaves
2 cloves of garlic
90g/3½oz butter
55g/2oz fresh coriander, chopped

Preheat the oven to 200°C/400°F/gas 6. Peel the plantains, cut into large pieces and cook gently in a pan with the olive oil. Add the thyme, garlic and half of the butter. Bake in the preheated oven for about 10 minutes. This will soften the plantains further. When ready, remove the plantains from the oven and mash with a fork. Add the rest of the butter and the chopped coriander.

# carrot purée

455g/1lb carrots
115g/4oz butter
55g/2oz sugar
½ teaspoon cumin seeds, crushed
salt and freshly ground black pepper

Wash and peel the carrots. Cut them into small pieces and place in a
pan with the butter and sugar. Cover with water and bring to the boil.
Leave to simmer until soft. Drain and put through a mouli or mash with
a fork. Add the cumin, correct the seasoning and serve.

see page 49 butternut squash and vegetable curry

see pages 54, 55, 56, 57 clockwise from top left garlic mashed potato; plantain mash; carrot purée; pumpkin purée

see pages 67, 68 french beans with chilli and ginger *bottom* french beans with red onion, coriander and mushrooms

see pages 75–8 left fresh saltfish and ackee; right roast red bream with chickpeas and pea froth

see page 86 deep-fried squid in curry batter

see page 80   baked snapper in fragrant spices with vegetables

see page 81 baked lobster with ackee and okra fricassee

see pages 95, 93 left stew chicken; right pat's roast chicken

# pumpkin purée

1 medium pumpkin
170g/6oz butter
1 teaspoon sugar
1 teaspoon freshly grated nutmeg
salt and freshly ground black pepper

Peel the pumpkin and cut into small pieces. Place in a pan with the
butter and sugar. Cover with water and bring to the boil. Leave to
simmer until soft, then drain, reserving the liquor. Put through a mouli,
or purée in a food processor, adding a little of the reserved cooking
liquor if the purée is too thick. Add the nutmeg, correct the seasoning
and serve.

# yam bubble and squeak

Yams are very versatile and part of the staple diet in the Caribbean. They can be treated in the same way as potatoes, so can be simply boiled, or used in bubble and squeak, as with this recipe. Yellow yams are very starchy and therefore perfect for this type of dish. However, they can also be extremely bitter, and are an acquired taste. Sweet potato can also be incorporated into this recipe if you fancy.

makes 4–6 cakes

140g/5oz white yam, peeled and halved
200g/7oz yellow yam, peeled and diced
2 spring onions, diced
1 chilli, diced
6 tablespoons olive oil
90g/3½oz tinned callaloo or spinach
2 tablespoons chopped fresh coriander
2 tablespoons chopped fresh parsley

Parboil the white yam for 5 minutes and leave to one side to cool. Cook the yellow yam until soft enough to mash. Soften the spring onions and chilli in half the olive oil and add the callaloo or spinach. Continue cooking for 2–3 minutes and then leave to cool.

Grate the white yam and add to the callaloo or spinach mixture. Stir in the herbs. Mix in the mashed yellow yam to bind the mixture. Make into cakes and gently fry on each side in the rest of the oil for 2–3 minutes or until golden brown. Serve as a vegetarian main dish or as a potato dish to accompany any main course.

# baked avocado surprise

This is a mouth-watering and unusual way of serving this popular fruit.

serves 2
1 red pepper, finely diced
1 Scotch bonnet chilli, finely diced
1 red onion, finely diced
2 spring onions, finely diced
olive oil
1 clove of garlic, crushed
2 avocados (not too ripe)
salt and freshly ground black pepper
a pinch of paprika

for the sauce
425ml/¾ pint milk
1 onion, studded with 4 cloves and 1 bay leaf
55g/2oz butter
55g/2oz flour, sifted
115g/4oz Gruyère cheese (or to taste), grated

To make the sauce, gently warm the milk and the studded onion in a pan. In another pan, melt the butter on a low heat and then gradually add the flour to make a roux. Now start to add the milk, stirring constantly to make sure there are no lumps. Cook the sauce for a further 5–10 minutes, until the floury taste disappears. Finish by adding the Gruyère cheese, and then leave to one side. I prefer my sauce to be quite thin, but if you prefer it to be thicker just use less milk.

Meanwhile, cook all the finely diced vegetables gently in a little oil with the crushed garlic. Cook until the vegetables are soft, then leave to one side to cool. Halve the avocados lengthways and remove the stones. Using a spoon, remove the avocado flesh without splitting the skin. Dice the avocado flesh, season with salt and pepper, and put it in a large bowl with the diced vegetable mixture. Add enough white sauce to bind the ingredients.

Preheat the oven to 190°C/375°F/gas 5. Lay the avocado skins in an ovenproof dish and pile in the filling. Bake in the preheated oven for 5 minutes, then remove from the oven, sprinkle with paprika and serve. A crisp mixed salad is a perfect accompaniment for my avocado surprise.

# deep-fried parsnips

serves 4

**2 parsnips, peeled and cut into strips**
**salt and freshly ground black pepper**
**vegetable oil for deep-frying**

Heat vegetable oil in a deep fat fryer, to 160°C/315°F. Drop the parsnips in and cook until golden brown. Remove from the oil and place on kitchen paper to soak up any excess oil. Season and serve. These parsnips go well with saltfish and ackee (see page 75).

# crispy leek

2 leeks
salt and freshly ground black pepper
vegetable oil for deep-frying

Remove all the dark green parts of the leeks and discard, then cut each leek in half lengthways. Cut these lengths in half again and then cut the leeks into thin julienne strips. Place in a colander and wash off any dirt. Heat oil in a deep fat fryer to 140°C/275°F. Dry the leeks and cook in the oil until crispy and golden brown. Remove from the oil and place on kitchen paper to drain off any excess oil. Season and serve. These are nice scattered over the top of roast red bream with chickpeas and pea froth (see page 78).

# steamed callaloo

Callaloo is the Caribbean alternative to spinach. It is the cornerstone of many West Indian diets, used in various dishes and also eaten as a vegetable in its own right. I have eaten freshly grown callaloo from England, but it tastes different from that grown in the Caribbean. It is found in abundance, tinned, at most large supermarkets or ethnic food stores but it can be very soft and mushy. I have opted to use spinach in most of my recipes because it is easy to find and fresh, where possible, is always best.

Here is a recipe for steamed callaloo, in case you find some of the lovely fresh leaves.

serves 2

a large bunch of callaloo leaves, stripped of fibre and chopped
100g/3½oz butter or margarine
3 spring onions, chopped
1 teaspoon chopped chilli
1 medium tomato, peeled, deseeded and chopped

Bring a pan of salted water to the boil. Add the callaloo and simmer for 2 minutes until the leaves are tender but still green, then drain. Melt the butter in a pan and sauté the spring onions and chilli. Add the tomato and cook until soft. Add the callaloo, toss well and serve.

# sautéed spinach

Fresh spinach is a beautiful vegetable – always use more than you think you will need, because it wilts so much during cooking. Spinach must be washed thoroughly, as it is normally very gritty and dirty. Adding a little salt to the water when washing it is a good idea, as it will kill any foreign bodies which may be attached to the leaves.

½ a small onion, diced
1 clove of garlic, crushed
3 tablespoons extra virgin olive oil
455g/1lb large leaf spinach, washed and picked
a pinch of freshly grated nutmeg
a pinch of cayenne
salt and freshly ground black pepper

Cook the onion and garlic in a little olive oil on a moderate heat until soft. Remove the garlic and onion, then add more olive oil to the pan and get it fairly hot. Add the spinach. Once it's in the pan, stir it continuously, making sure the leaves do not get crushed. Once the leaves have wilted, stir in the onion and garlic, season with the spices, salt and pepper, and serve.

# blanched spinach

When blanching spinach, it is very important not to overcook it – you want to keep as many vitamins in the spinach as possible. This means keeping the leaves as green as you can so the optimum nutritional value can be acquired from the dish.

455g/1lb spinach, washed and picked
salt and freshly ground black pepper
a pinch of freshly grated nutmeg
115g/4oz butter

Bring a large pan of salted water to the boil and add the spinach in two batches, making sure the leaves are removed from the water once they wilt. If the spinach is to be served immediately, drain well, season with salt, pepper and nutmeg, add butter, and serve. But if it is for later use, plunge it immediately into ice-cold water and then drain, squeezing out any excess water. Refrigerate for up to 2 days. To use, simply reheat in a little butter.

# blanched french beans

French beans are a wonderful fresh green vegetable which I tend to use as an alternative to the traditional runner bean. Available all year round, they are very easy to cook and very versatile. Not boring at all!

serves 4–6

455g/1lb French beans
salt and freshly ground black pepper

Top and tail the beans. Plunge into boiling salted water a few at a time, without letting the water come off the boil. Cook for 6–8 minutes, then drain, season and serve.

# french beans with chilli and ginger

serves 4–6

Prepare and cook the beans as in the blanched beans recipe (see page 66). Warm 1 teaspoon of olive oil in a pan and add 2 teaspoons of chopped red chilli and ½ teaspoon of chopped fresh ginger. Cook gently for a couple of minutes, then add the beans and toss until well coated. Season well, drain any excess oil and serve.

# french beans with red onion, coriander and mushrooms

serves 4–6

Prepare and cook the beans as in the blanched beans recipe (see page 66). Put 115g/4oz of sliced or torn mushrooms, 8–10 leaves of coriander and 1 chopped small red onion in a pan with a little olive oil and cook gently for a couple of minutes. Mix well with the beans.

# butter melted cabbage

A really tasty vegetable dish, which comes with its own buttery juices.
Beautiful with steamed fish.

serves 4

140g/5oz butter
1 clove of garlic, crushed
1 bay leaf
1 tablespoon fresh thyme leaves
1 tablespoon pimento seeds, crushed
1 tablespoon black peppercorns, crushed
1 medium white cabbage, sliced
grated zest of 1 lemon
salt and freshly ground black pepper

Put the butter into a large pan and heat. Add the garlic, herbs and
spices and cook gently for 5–8 minutes, being careful not to let the
butter burn. Add the cabbage and lemon zest. Place a lid on the pan
and just leave on a low heat for the cabbage to stew down into all that
flavour. This will take about 10 minutes. Season well and serve.

# stir-fried spring greens

olive oil
400g/14oz shredded spring greens
2 red chillies, deseeded and thinly sliced
4 spring onions, stalks shredded, bulbs left whole
1 clove of garlic, sliced
140g/5oz beansprouts
3 tablespoons sweet chilli sauce
a handful of fresh coriander, chopped

Heat the oil in a stir-fry pan. Add the spring greens and stir-fry for 3–4 minutes. Add the chillies, spring onions and garlic and cook for 1 minute. Add the beansprouts and chilli sauce, then the chopped coriander. Serve immediately.

# summer vegetable tower

serves 4

1 small butternut squash, peeled, deseeded and quartered
6 sprigs of fresh thyme, leaves picked
2 cloves of garlic, sliced
8 tablespoons pimento oil (see page 189)
salt and freshly ground black pepper
a handful of shelled broad beans
a handful of mustard leaves
a handful of watercress
4 tablespoons sherry vinegar
1 large beef tomato
½ a christophene, peeled and thinly sliced
1 carrot, peeled and thinly sliced

Preheat the oven to 180°C/350°F/gas 4. Put the squash, thyme and garlic on a roasting tray with the pimento oil and cook in the oven for about 10 minutes, being careful not to let the squash get too soft. Leave to cool, then season well and cut into bite-size pieces. Cook the broad beans in boiling water for 3–4 minutes. Refresh in ice-cold water and drain, then remove the skins.

Put the roasted squash, beans, mustard leaves and watercress in a bowl with the pimento oil from the roasting tray. Add the sherry vinegar, season and mix well.

Skin and slice the beef tomato and arrange one slice at the base of the salad plate. Build up a small tower with the leaves and the cooked and raw vegetables.

# seafood

Like most islanders, those of the Caribbean enjoy fish as the basis of their staple diet. How lucky to have such a versatile food available all year round!

In this chapter, I've purposely stuck to using fish from British shores or the Med, simply for the ease of obtaining it fresh. Fish which has been frozen or ice-packed during freight from other shores is just not the same. My advice would be to find yourself a reliable fishmonger. The key to successful cooking is having the best raw ingredients to work with, so it makes sense to have the freshest seafood possible.

I love all seafood, but I am especially fond of shellfish. Crab is my absolute favourite – a very versatile crustacean, but best when simply served with a little lemon or lime juice or a touch of mayonnaise to enhance its flavour. You'll also find two recipes using crab in the Salad chapter.

# fried king fish with fresh jangas and boiled green bananas

Jangas is the Caribbean word for king prawns.

55g/2oz plain flour
dried fish seasoning
salt and freshly ground black pepper
2 x 170g/6oz king fish, on the bone
200ml/7fl oz vegetable oil
8 fresh king prawns, peeled
2 sweet red peppers, sliced
1 Scotch bonnet chilli, sliced
2 tomatoes, sliced
1 spring onion, sliced
115g/4oz butter
3 green bananas

Mix the flour with the fish seasoning, salt and pepper. Dust the fish with the seasoned flour. Heat a frying-pan until very hot. Add the oil and carefully brown the fish – this should take 3–4 minutes. Remove the fish from the pan, add the prawns and cook for 1 minute. Add all the vegetables and the butter and cook until soft. Peel the green bananas and place in a pan of boiling salted water. Cook for 10 minutes. Drain the bananas and leave to cool. Then slice at an angle. Add the fish to the vegetables, reheat and serve with the bananas.

# fresh saltfish and ackee

Saltfish and ackee is *the* dish of the Caribbean as well as being one of the most popular. This is my interpretation using fresh cod steaks. You will need to prepare the cod 24 hours before cooking.

serves 4

140g/5oz rock salt
4 x 225g/8oz cod steaks
½ tablespoon freshly ground black pepper
1 tablespoon ground pimento seeds
2 tablespoons olive oil
1 onion, finely diced
2 Scotch bonnet chillies, diced
2 spring onions, sliced
2 cloves of garlic, crushed
1 x 400g/14oz tin of ackee
2 tomatoes, sliced
2 tablespoons tomato fondue (see page 167)

Use all the rock salt to cover the cod steaks and leave in the fridge for at least 6–8 hours. When you are ready to cook it, rinse thoroughly and drain the fish. Dry it with clean kitchen paper. Season the cod with a sprinkle of black pepper and half a teaspoon of ground pimento. Be sure not to use any more salt.

Heat a large pan and add the olive oil. Cook the cod steaks two at a time, until they are golden brown on both sides. This should take 3–4 minutes on each side.

When all the cod steaks are done, place them on a greased baking tray and put in the oven on a low heat to keep them warm. Add the onion, Scotch bonnets, spring onions and garlic to the frying-pan and sauté until they start to colour.

Add the drained ackee and sliced tomatoes to the pan and season with the remaining black pepper and ground pimento. Be careful not to break up the ackees, as they break apart easily. In a separate pan, gently warm the tomato fondue.

To serve, place the cod on a plate topped with tomato fondue and some ackee mixture. This classic Caribbean dish is worthy of any dinner table.

# fried 'seasoned' black bream

This dish reminds me of the fried fish I ate as a child with pickled vegetables (see page 41) and doorstep pieces of bread, washed down with a large glass of carrot juice (see page 143). The fish needs to be seasoned 24 hours before cooking.

serves 4

4 x 455–680g/1–1½lb whole bream
2 teaspoons black peppercorns, crushed
4 teaspoons cumin seeds, crushed
1 teaspoon pimento seeds, crushed
1 teaspoon coriander seeds, crushed
2 teaspoons rock salt
1 Scotch bonnet chilli, very finely chopped, or 1 teaspoon chilli powder
140g/5oz plain flour, seasoned
140ml/5fl oz vegetable oil
pickled vegetables (see page 41)
a handful of fresh flat-leaf parsley, chopped

Ask your fishmonger to scale and gut the fish, trim any fins and remove the gills. This way, once the fish is cooked, everything can be eaten. All the hard work for this dish will then be done – everything else is simple.

Season the fish with the spices, salt and chilli 24 hours before it is to be cooked. When ready to cook, score the fish with a sharp filleting knife on both sides, then lightly dust with seasoned flour. Fry in hot oil, making sure that the fish does not become too dry – this should take about 3 minutes on each side. The skin of the fish should be crispy and the flesh moist.

Remove from the pan, place on kitchen paper to absorb excess fat, and serve with a generous helping of pickled vegetables and chopped parsley.

# roast red bream with chickpeas and pea froth

This dish, if well planned, will take hardly any time at all.

serves 4

4 tablespoons olive oil
½ an onion, peeled and sliced
1 clove of garlic
140g/5oz fresh or frozen peas
water or stock
4 x 140g/5oz red bream fillets
salt and freshly ground black pepper
1 tablespoon saffron
55ml/2fl oz double cream, whipped
a knob of butter
1 x chickpeas recipe (see page 118)
2 tablespoons chopped fresh coriander

To make the pea froth, heat 1 tablespoon of the olive oil in a pan, add the onion and garlic, and cook until soft. Add the peas and cook for a further minute. Add enough water or stock to cover the peas and bring to the boil. Liquidize, pass through a strainer, and set aside.

To cook the fish, heat the rest of the olive oil in a frying-pan. Season the fish fillets with salt, pepper and saffron on the skin side only – this will enhance both the flavour and the colour. Cook the fish for 2 minutes on each side. At the last minute, just before serving, add the whipped cream and butter to the peas. Use a hand blender or whisk to create a frothy cappuccino effect.

Serve the fish on top of the pea froth and chickpeas, garnished with coriander.

# roast fillets of cod with spiced vegetables

serves 4

8 small whole spring onions
8 stems of baby fennel
3 red peppers
2 plum tomatoes
4 x 140g/5oz cod fillets
salt and freshly ground black pepper
1 teaspoon paprika
3 tablespoons olive oil
2 cloves of garlic, sliced
1 teaspoon chopped fresh ginger
a pinch of saffron
600ml/22fl oz fish stock
3 tablespoons chopped fresh coriander

If using larger spring onions, cut in half. Blanch the spring onions for 1–2 minutes and refresh in cold water. Cook the fennel stems in boiling, salted water for 3–4 minutes and refresh, leaving to one side. With a blowtorch or over an open flame on the stove, blister the skin on the peppers and place in a bowl. Place clingfilm over the bowl while the peppers are hot, and the skins will steam off. Deseed the peppers and cut into pieces.

Blanch, peel and deseed the tomatoes, and cut the flesh into large chunks. Dust the cod with black pepper and paprika and set aside.

Heat the olive oil in a thick-bottomed pan and fry the garlic and ginger. Add the fennel, spring onions and saffron, and cook for 2 minutes. Add the stock and simmer until the liquid has reduced by half. Add the peppers, tomatoes and coriander.

Cook the cod in a little olive oil for 3 minutes on each side. Arrange the vegetables on a serving plate with the fish on top.

# baked snapper in fragrant spices with vegetables

The essence of this dish is, again, in the marinating. You will need to let the fish marinate for 12–24 hours.

serves 2

2 x 455g/1lb whole red snapper
1 lime
2 teaspoons coriander seeds, crushed
2 teaspoons black peppercorns, crushed
1 cinnamon stick, crushed
2 teaspoons pimento seeds, crushed
a pinch of rock salt
4 tablespoons olive oil
1 avocado, peeled and sliced into 8 pieces
1 christophene, peeled, cut into slices and blanched briefly
2 red onions, cut in 1cm/½ inch thick rings
1 tablespoon chopped garlic
1 tablespoon chopped fresh ginger
1 bulb of fennel, sliced in 1cm/½ inch thick rings
2 red peppers, quartered
1 Scotch bonnet chilli, finely chopped
1 small bunch of fresh coriander, chopped

Ask your fishmonger to scale, gut and de-gill the fish for you. Wash the fish thoroughly and then rub with one half of the lime. Score the fish on both sides and rub generously with the ground spices and salt. Let the fish marinate for 12–24 hours. When you are ready to cook the fish, preheat the oven to 180°C/350°F/gas 4. Get a pan hot, add some olive oil and cook the fish until golden brown on both sides. Place in an ovenproof dish and bake in the preheated oven for about 10 minutes.

Heat plenty of olive oil in a pan and cook the avocado until brown. Remove from the pan and set aside. Add the christophene, then the onions, garlic, ginger and fennel. Cook for a few minutes, then add the red peppers and Scotch bonnet. When all the vegetables are golden brown, add the chopped coriander and return the avocado to the pan. Serve immediately, with the fish.

# baked lobster with ackee and okra fricassee

This dish looks amazing and has a beautiful combination of flavours. Elegantly presented, it's a real winner!

serves 4

4 x 450g/1lb Canadian or Scotch lobsters
1 x court-bouillon recipe (see page 161)
1 large red onion, finely diced
4 cloves of garlic, thinly sliced
½ a Scotch bonnet chilli, finely chopped
a pinch of saffron
a pinch of curry powder
5 tablespoons olive oil
5 tablespoons tomato fondue (see page 167)
140g/5oz okra
1 x 400g/14oz tin of ackee, drained
salt and freshly ground black pepper
2 tablespoons chopped fresh flat-leaf parsley

Poach the lobsters in the court-bouillon for about 5 minutes. When cooked, remove from the liquor and leave to cool.

In a thick-bottomed pan cook the onion, garlic, Scotch bonnet, saffron and curry powder in a little olive oil until the vegetables are nicely coloured. Stir in the tomato fondue.

Top, tail and wash the okra. Blanch for about 2 minutes. Remove from the water, refresh and roughly chop. Add the okra and ackee to the other vegetables in the pan and leave to simmer for 4–5 minutes. Season, and sprinkle with the parsley.

Remove the claws from the lobsters and split the bodies in half lengthways. Remove all the flesh and discard the debris from the head. Wash out the body shell. Crack the claws open and remove the claw meat, discarding the shells. Slice up all the flesh. Fill the body shells with the ackee and okra mix. Top this with warm sliced pieces of lobster. Place on a baking tray and warm in the oven for 5 minutes at 200°C/400°F/gas 6. Serve with a crisp salad of leaves and herbs.

# seared blackened salmon with a coriander yoghurt dressing

This wonderful dish is very easy to prepare, has fabulous flavours, and is great at setting off smoke alarms!

serves 4

2 cucumbers
salt
4 x 140g/5oz salmon fillets
1 teaspoon white peppercorns, freshly ground
1 teaspoon black peppercorns, freshly ground
30g/1oz garlic powder
1 teaspoon chilli powder (or to taste)
55ml/2fl oz olive oil
155ml/5½fl oz yoghurt
2 small sprigs of fresh coriander, finely chopped
mixed salad leaves

Wash and peel the cucumbers, and cut them into thirds. Using a mandolin, cut them into thin strips 2cm/1 inch wide, making sure there are no seeds in the cucumber slices. Lightly sprinkle with salt and leave to one side.

Score the skin side of the salmon, and coat each piece with the ground spices. Heat the oil in a frying-pan, and when hot enough place the salmon fillets skin-side down for approximately 3–4 minutes, or until the spices have blackened. Turn and cook for a further 2 minutes on the other side.

Squeeze any excess water from the salted cucumbers, and mix with the yoghurt and half the coriander. To serve, put a good dollop of the yoghurt dressing in the middle of each plate, place the salmon on top, and drizzle any remaining dressing over the dish. Sprinkle with the rest of the chopped coriander and serve with a mixed leaf salad.

# sardines in a cornmeal crust with mixed leaves and pepper frenzy salsa

Fresh sardines are one of the best things ever. For me they bring back memories of fishermen trying to sell their catch of the day on the beach, and me choosing the freshly caught sardines. Once home, I would sprinkle water over them before gently roasting on flavoured barks and wood chippings.

Any good fishmonger will prepare sardines properly for you, making sure they are scaled and gutted. Just ask him to do this when you buy them.

serves 2

8 x 70g/2½oz sardines
salt and freshly ground black pepper
1 dessertspoon grain mustard
115g/4oz cornmeal
extra virgin olive oil
a handful of rocket
a handful of curly endive
1 x pepper frenzy salsa recipe (see page 172)

Score and season the sardines, brush them all over with mustard and roll them in the cornmeal. Heat a frying-pan, add some extra virgin olive oil, and gently fry the sardines until the cornmeal is golden brown. Wash the salad leaves and arrange them on serving plates. Place a couple of sardines on top of this, sprinkle with salsa and serve.

# red mullet escabeche

It is alleged that this particular dish was brought to the Caribbean by the Portuguese. It has quite a European feel to it.

serves 4

285ml/½ pint water
2 red onions, thinly sliced
3 carrots, thinly sliced
4 black peppercorns
4 pimento seeds
3 cloves of garlic
1 bay leaf
1 tablespoon fresh thyme leaves
8 tablespoons sherry vinegar
4 tablespoons olive oil
4 x 140g/5oz fillets of red mullet
salt and freshly ground black pepper

Bring the water to the boil, then add the onions, carrots, peppercorns, pimento seeds, garlic, bay leaf and thyme. Cook for about 15 minutes. Leave to cool, then add the vinegar and olive oil. Heat a little olive oil in a frying-pan and cook the fish on both sides – be careful not to overcook. Place the fish on a plate and pour the vegetables and liquor over. It can be served hot or cold.

# fried red mullet with sweet potato chips and garlic mayonnaise

For me there is no other fish quite like red mullet. Always very small, once fried you can eat the whole fish – head to tail! Ask your fishmonger to scale and gut the fish for you.

serves 4

1 x mayonnaise recipe (page 179), adding 1 clove of crushed garlic
1 teaspoon paprika
1 teaspoon coriander seeds, ground
a pinch of ground ginger
1 teaspoon curry powder
freshly ground black pepper
1 teaspoon fresh thyme leaves, chopped
2 tablespoons flour
2 sweet potatoes
vegetable oil for deep-frying
8 x 115g/4oz red mullet
olive oil

Make the mayonnaise, adding a crushed clove of garlic with the egg yolks and mustard. Mix the spices and thyme with the flour. Parboil the sweet potatoes in salted water for about 10 minutes. Refresh in cold water, slice into chips (finger-width) and deep-fry in oil until golden brown. Meanwhile, wash the mullet thoroughly and pat dry with kitchen paper. Lightly dust with the seasoned flour. Gently heat a little olive oil in a pan and fry each fish for 4–5 minutes. Don't let the oil get too hot. When ready, remove the fish from the oil and drain on kitchen paper.

Serve the fish with the sweet potato chips and a good dollop of garlic mayonnaise on the side.

# deep-fried squid in curry batter

Squid can be found in any supermarket or at your local fishmonger's. If buying from the fishmonger, ask for it to be cleaned and left as tubes. The squid needs to be marinated for 12 hours before cooking.

serves 2

2 medium squid tubes
juice of 2 lemons
1 tablespoon fresh thyme leaves
2 cloves of garlic, crushed
6 tablespoons olive oil
plain flour, seasoned with salt, pepper and curry powder
paprika

for the curry batter

3oz/85g butter
2 teaspoons curry powder
85g/3oz cornflour
85g/3oz sifted plain flour
salt and freshly ground black pepper
200ml/7fl oz lager
1 egg yolk
15g/½oz fresh yeast

Put the squid in a bowl with the lemon juice, thyme, garlic and a little olive oil. Leave to marinate for up to 12 hours.

Melt the butter in a pan and fry the curry powder gently. Place in a bowl. Add the cornflour and plain flour with some salt and pepper and make a well in the centre. Add the lager gradually, whisking all the time. You should have a beautiful lump-free batter. Stir in the egg yolk and the yeast. Cover with clingfilm and put in a warm place.

Heat oil for deep-frying to 180°C/350°F. Cut the squid tubes into 0.5cm/¼ inch rings. Dip each one first into the seasoned flour then into the batter, and fry for about 1–2 minutes or until golden brown. When ready, drain on kitchen paper and dust with paprika.

# caribbean crabcake

170g/6oz cold mashed potato
4 egg yolks
salt and freshly ground black pepper
2 tablespoons brown crabmeat
1 Scotch bonnet chilli, finely diced
2 tablespoons finely diced red onion
50g/1¾oz butter
170g/6oz white crabmeat
1 tablespoon chopped fresh parsley
1 tablespoon chopped fresh chives
juice of 1 lime
3 slices of white bread, crusts removed
90g/3½oz flour
olive oil

Put the mashed potato in a bowl, add the egg yolks and beat well.
Season well, and fold in the brown crabmeat.

Soften the Scotch bonnet and red onion in the butter and leave to
cool. Add the white crabmeat, herbs, lime juice and cooled vegetables.
Gently mix until all the ingredients are well combined.

At this stage, see how wet the mixture is. Crumb the bread and add
enough to make the mixture firm. Mould into cakes, dusting your
hands with flour so the mixture doesn't stick.

Preheat the oven to 200°C/400°F/gas 6. Heat some oil in a pan. Lightly
flour the crabcakes and fry gently on each side until golden brown.
Transfer to the preheated oven and cook for 8–10 minutes. Serve with
a crisp salad.

# sautéed prawns

24 raw medium prawns
2 tablespoons olive oil
1 onion, finely diced
2 cloves of garlic, chopped
2 chillies, finely diced
1 teaspoon sugar
155ml/5½fl oz fish stock
2 tomatoes, chopped
1 clove
salt and freshly ground black pepper
juice of 1–2 limes
1 tablespoon chopped fresh parsley
1 tablespoon chopped fresh chives

Peel the prawns and remove the sac from the back using a sharp knife. Gently heat the oil in a frying-pan. Quick-fry the prawns until they are partially red, then remove from the pan.

Add the onion, garlic and chilli, cook for about 1 minute, and add the sugar. Let this gently caramelize. Add the fish stock to the pan and reduce the liquid by half. Add the diced tomatoes and clove to the sauce. Let this simmer for a further 2–3 minutes. Add the prawns. Season.

Squeeze the lime juice into the sauce; you need enough to flavour, so taste as you add it. Sprinkle with the chopped herbs.

# meat

I love eating meat. However, about two years ago I tried cutting it out of my diet and just ate fish. Curried goat became my only vice – I can't resist it when my mum or aunts make it. However, it all went pear-shaped and I ended up eating all kinds of meat after all: jerk pork, jerk chicken, oxtail stew, the lot. I cannot do without my favourite meat dishes.

The recipes in this chapter are all things I grew up eating at home – flavours I've never forgotten. I'm a firm believer that food and flavours that give you comfort as a child remain in your adult subconscious. Certain smells and tastes will trigger certain memories. With these recipes I am trying to relive my happy, fun-filled youth, watching my grandmother cooking a magnificent meaty feast – which was almost every day! And I hope that they will give you a taste of my Caribbean upbringing.

# curried shank of lamb with couscous

A lamb shank is a wonderful cut of meat, ideal for one portion. The meat needs to be seasoned 6–8 hours in advance.

serves 4

4 lamb shanks
3 dessertspoons curry powder
1 teaspoon fresh or dried thyme
1 teaspoon ground pimento seeds
1 teaspoon saffron
2 teaspoons freshly ground black pepper
2 teaspoons coriander seeds, crushed
140ml/5fl oz vegetable oil
4 tomatoes, chopped
2 onions, finely diced
2 red peppers, finely diced
2 cloves of garlic, chopped
olive oil
90g/3½oz coconut cream
4 litres/7 pints water or stock
1 x couscous recipe (see page 117)

Season the lamb with the curry powder, thyme, pimento, saffron, black pepper and coriander seeds at least 6–8 hours before using. When ready to cook, preheat the oven to 150°C/300°F/gas 2. Heat the oil in a pan and cook the shanks until golden brown. Place the shanks in a large thick-bottomed pan. Soften the tomatoes, onions, peppers and garlic in some olive oil and add to the lamb. Add the coconut cream and water or stock and bring to the boil. Remove the pan from the heat and cook in the preheated oven for 1–1½ hours, until the lamb is tender. When ready, remove the lamb from the pan, simmer the sauce till reduced by half, then return the meat to the pan and serve with couscous.

# lemon and thyme lamb shanks

To me, lamb shanks are one of the most succulent stewing cuts. You
will need to let the lamb marinate for 6–8 hours. This recipe, like the
previous one, is really nice served with couscous.

serves 4

8 cloves of garlic, sliced
1 large bunch of fresh thyme, leaves picked
90g/3½oz rock salt
4 lamb shanks
8 black peppercorns, crushed
2kg/4½lb duck fat
4 lemons
3 tablespoons honey

Pound half the garlic and half the thyme leaves with the rock salt and
spread over the meat. Leave to marinate for 6–8 hours.

Make small incisions in the lamb and slip pieces of the remaining
garlic into the incisions. Brown the lamb in a very hot frying-pan,
adding the black peppercorns. When the lamb is golden brown,
remove and place in a thick-bottomed casserole or pan. Cover with the
duck fat and the juice of 2 of the lemons and set aside. Place the lemon
halves in the pan and add the rest of the thyme.

Preheat the oven to 150°C/300°F/gas 2 and cook for about 60–90
minutes. When the lamb is done, heat the honey and remaining
lemon juice in a frying-pan. When they begin to caramelize, pour over
the lamb.

# coconut chicken

This dish is glorious – full of Caribbean flavour, and very impressive for dinner parties or other special occasions. The chicken needs to be marinated for at least 24 hours.

serves 6–8
1 free-range chicken, jointed into 8 pieces
vinegar
lemon juice
140ml/¼ pint vegetable oil
plain flour
3 tablespoons honey
1 small fresh coconut, grated
1 small bunch of fresh coriander, chopped

for the marinade
3 teaspoons pimento seeds, crushed
2 cloves garlic, crushed
3 teaspoons freshly ground black pepper
1 teaspoon coriander seeds, crushed
1 Scotch bonnet chilli, finely chopped
2 teaspoons rock salt

Wash the chicken pieces in a solution of vinegar, lemon and water – this will get rid of the funny taste that chicken can sometimes have. Dry on kitchen paper and place in a bowl with all the marinade ingredients. Leave for a minimum of 24 hours.

Preheat the oven to 180°C/350°F/gas 4. Heat a frying-pan and add the vegetable oil. Lightly flour the chicken and cook until golden brown on all sides. Now place the chicken on a baking tray, and bake in the preheated oven for 20–30 minutes. When almost ready, remove from the oven and coat the chicken with honey. Sprinkle over the coconut pieces and return the tray to the oven for another few minutes. Remove, and serve sprinkled with chopped coriander.

# pat's roast chicken

I love roast chicken – it's simple, tasty and you can leave it alone to cook in the oven. I use the particular spices in this recipe to bring alive a good old roast chicken. Leave it to marinate for about 4 hours if you can.

serves 4

1 x 1.4–1.8kg/3–4lb free-range chicken
vinegar
lemon juice
3 cloves of garlic, crushed
1 small bunch of fresh thyme
1 onion, halved
55g/2oz butter
115g/4oz jerk butter (see page 186)
1 tablespoon dried chicken seasoning
1 tablespoon turmeric
juice of 1 lime
salt and freshly ground black pepper
1 small bunch of fresh coriander, chopped

Wash the chicken thoroughly with a mix of vinegar, lemon juice and water. Put the garlic, thyme, onion and butter inside the chicken cavity. Gently separate the skin from the breasts and push the jerk butter into the space. Not only will it give the chicken a lovely flavour, it will keep the breast meat moist. Rub the chicken seasoning, turmeric, lime juice, salt and pepper over the chicken skin. Leave for 4 hours or as long as you can before cooking. Preheat the oven to 200°C/400°F/gas 6.

Place the chicken in a hot roasting tray, cover with foil and cook in the preheated oven for about an hour. Remove the foil after 30 minutes to let the chicken get golden brown.

Finish with chopped coriander and serve with rice and peas (see page 114).

# stuffing for roast chicken

Here is a great alternative to the one given in the previous recipe.

3 tablespoons olive oil
115g/4oz chicken livers
1 onion, diced
2 sticks of celery, chopped
55g/2oz butter
8–10 slices of stale bread
½ teaspoon ground pimento seeds
½ teaspoon freshly ground black pepper
salt
425ml/¾ pint water or chicken stock

Heat the oil in a frying-pan and sauté the chicken livers for a couple of minutes. Remove from the heat and drain. Add the vegetables to the pan with the butter, and when softened, return the livers to the pan, then remove from the heat. Blitz the bread in a food processor and add to the livers with the pimento and black pepper. Season. Place back on a low heat and add stock or water until the mixture comes together and makes a delicious stuffing.

# stew chicken

In the Caribbean a tougher, older bird would actually be used to make
this dish ('old boilers', I call them), but you can use any chicken you
like. Preferably free-range. You need to season the chicken 2 hours
before using.

serves 6

1 free-range chicken, jointed into 8 pieces
4 tablespoons pimento oil (see page 189)
90g/3½oz seasoned plain flour
1 clove of garlic, finely chopped
1 teaspoon finely diced fresh ginger
1 large onion, peeled and finely chopped
1 large carrot, peeled and diced
55g/2oz butter
1 chicken stock cube (optional)
850ml/1½ pints water or chicken stock
1 large potato, peeled and diced
1 beef tomato, peeled and diced
2 teaspoons fresh thyme leaves

for the spice rub

1 teaspoon turmeric
1 teaspoon curry powder
1 teaspoon cayenne
2 tablespoons crushed pimento seeds
1 teaspoon freshly ground black pepper
a pinch of ground cumin

Mix the spice rub ingredients together. Rub into the chicken pieces
and leave for 2 hours. When you are ready to cook, heat the oil in a
deep-sided pan. Dust the chicken with the seasoned flour and fry in
the oil until golden brown. Remove the chicken from the pan.

Add the garlic, ginger, onion and carrot to the pan with the butter
and cook for 2–3 minutes. Crumble in the stock cube and add the water

(or use chicken stock if you have some). Replace the chicken and continue to cook for 15 minutes. Now add the potato and cook for a further 10 minutes, or until the chicken is cooked. Finish by adding the tomatoes and thyme. Leave to infuse for 5 minutes and serve with rice and peas (see page 114).

# roast breast of duck with confit duck legs

The method of confit is an age-old one. The French have always used confits, both for preservation and the wonderful flavour it gives to food cooked in this way. Confit is normally used for large tough cuts of meat, or for poultry or game. Some chefs use confit for fish, but this takes much more skill. I am sure that this method is used in the Caribbean, especially as there are so many French-speaking islands, but I've yet to come across an authentic Caribbean recipe. Here's one of my own favourites.

You need to leave the duck legs in salt for 24 hours before cooking.

serves 2
1 x 2kg/4½lb duck
rock salt
thyme
455g/1lb duck or goose fat
mango salsa (see page 175, omitting the crabmeat)

for the spice bag
1 piece of muslin
2 nutmegs, crushed
4 pimento seeds
2 cinnamon sticks
2 star anise
4 black peppercorns
4 cloves of garlic
1 vanilla pod
zest of 1 orange

Remove the legs from the duck, cover with rock salt mixed with thyme, and leave for 24 hours. The salt will draw the moisture out of the skin and the thyme will give the duck a lovely flavour. Tie all the spice bag ingredients up in the muslin.

Preheat the oven to 150°C/300°F/gas 2. Brush off any salt left on the duck legs, and pour away any water which has been drawn from the skins. Pat the duck dry with kitchen paper. Put the duck legs into a deep pan and add the duck fat and the spice bag. Gently heat until the fat starts to simmer. Put the pan into the preheated oven and cook for 45–60 minutes. Remove from the oven and leave to cool. Turn the oven up to 200°C/400°F/gas 6.

Place the duck crown into a hot frying-pan with a little of the duck fat and colour the breasts. When golden brown, transfer to a roasting tray and place in the oven for about 15 minutes. Half-way through this time, place the duck legs in the same tray so that the fat really crisps up.

Remove the duck from the oven and serve with crown intact or with breasts removed, and with a big dollop of mango salsa.

# confit belly pork

Another great confit recipe. The belly pork needs to be marinated for up to 12 hours.

serves 8
1 side of belly pork, cut into 8 pieces
150g/5½oz rock salt
1 bunch of fresh thyme, leaves picked
10 pimento seeds, crushed
4 black peppercorns, crushed
4 cloves of garlic, sliced
2kg/4½lb duck fat

for the spice bag
1 piece of muslin
4 cloves
½ a bulb of garlic
90g/3½oz fresh ginger
zest of 1 orange
zest of 1 lime
1 cinnamon stick
1 nutmeg, crushed

With a knife, make little incisions all over the pork. Rub the salt, thyme, pimento and peppercorns into the meat, then stuff the garlic into the incisions. Leave to marinate for 12 hours.

Tie all the spice bag ingredients up in the muslin. Preheat the oven to 150°C/300°F/gas 2.

Wash the marinade from the pork and pat dry. Fry the meat in a hot frying-pan until golden brown on all sides. Place in a thick-bottomed pan with the spice bag and cover with the duck fat. Cook in the preheated oven for about 45–60 minutes. When ready, remove the meat from the fat and serve with stir-fried spring greens and barbecue sauce (see pages 70 and 165). Absolutely delicious.

# chinese pork

The marinade used here is lovely and sweet. It works perfectly with pork. The pork needs to be marinated for 12 hours.

serves 8
1 side of belly pork, cut into 8 pieces
3 tablespoons pimento oil (see page 189)

for the marinade
2 tablespoons rock salt
10 pimento seeds, crushed
4 black peppercorns, crushed
3 cloves of garlic
2 tablespoons honey
4 tablespoons soy sauce
2 tablespoons Chinese five-spice
1 tablespoon sweet chilli sauce
1 tablespoon chopped fresh ginger
2 tablespoons chopped fresh coriander

Liquidize the marinade ingredients. Coat the meat in the marinade and leave for 12 hours. Preheat the oven to 190°C/375°F/gas 5. Heat the pimento oil in a roasting tray and brown the pork pieces. Pour the marinade over the pork and put into the preheated oven for about 1 hour. Keep basting the pork and turning the pieces of meat until all sides are coated, sticky and golden brown. If the sauce reduces too much in the pan, add a little water.

Serve with stir-fried egg noodles (see page 121).

# roast rib of pork

The meat will need to be marinated for 24–48 hours before cooking.

serves 4
1 x 4-bone rack of pork
rock salt
4 cloves of garlic, crushed
1 small bunch of thyme, leaves picked
10 pimento seeds, crushed
4 tablespoons olive oil
140ml/5fl oz orange juice
140ml/5fl oz sherry vinegar

for the mirepoix vegetables
1 large onion, chopped
1 large carrot, chopped
1 bulb of garlic, cloves separated
1 leek, sliced
1 small bunch of fresh thyme, leaves picked
2 beef tomatoes, chopped

Lightly salt the pork, then stuff a clove of garlic into each section with some thyme and pimento. Leave to marinate for up to 48 hours. Preheat the oven to 220°C/425°F/gas 7 and get a roasting tray really hot. Add the oil, put the pork in the tray, place on the heat and brown on every side. Remove from the tray and brown the mirepoix vegetables. Place the joint back on top of the vegetables and cook in the preheated oven for 45–60 minutes, until tender.

In a separate pan, simmer the orange juice and sherry vinegar till reduced, use this to baste the joint throughout cooking – this will give it a beautiful sweet and sour flavour.

# roast rib eye of beef

Beef is the king of all meats in my opinion, and this is a fabulous way to cook it. Ask your local butcher to bone it but tie the bone back on to the meat during cooking to prevent it shrinking. We also want to use the juicy ribs for a barbecue nibble while we make the veg.

serves 6–8

1 x 4kg/9lb joint of beef
rock salt
8 black peppercorns, crushed
6 pimento seeds, crushed
3 tablespoons pimento oil (see page 189)
1 small bunch of fresh thyme
1 bulb of garlic, halved crosswise
1 x barbecue sauce recipe (see page 165)

Preheat the oven to 190°C/375°F/gas 5. Season the beef with salt, black pepper and pimento seeds. Heat the pimento oil in a roasting tray and seal the meat on all sides to keep in all that flavour. Place the beef fat-side down, add the thyme and garlic to the tray and place in the oven.

Keep basting the joint throughout the cooking process. A joint of this size will take about 2 hours to cook medium rare. If you want the joint well done, then cook it for 2 hours 45 minutes. Half-way through cooking, remove the joint from the oven and remove the bones. Cut them into ribs, coat them with barbecue sauce and place on a separate baking sheet in the oven for 15 minutes. Put the joint back in the oven for the rest of the cooking time.

When the spare ribs are ready you can either munch away on your own – they are absolutely delicious – or wait and serve them with the beef. Remove the beef from the oven and leave it somewhere warm to rest for about half an hour before serving.

For some tasty roast vegetables, add them to the roasting tray while the beef is resting. Red onions, potatoes and breadfruit are all great cooked in the meat juices. They will take about 20 minutes.

# boiled beef served with island vegetables

This is a wonderful one-pot dish, a classic style of Caribbean cookery. You will need to make sure that the vegetables are added to the broth at the right time and that they're not over-cooked.

Ask your local butcher and he will obtain a piece of salt brisket for you. Some meats need to be soaked in water for 12–24 hours if over-salted – speak to your butcher and he will set you straight on how salty the beef is. It is very important not to use more salt during cooking.

'serves 4–6
1 x 905g–1.4kg/2–3lb piece of brisket beef, salted
4 large carrots, roughly chopped
2 large onions, roughly chopped
1 bulb of garlic, roughly chopped
3 sticks of celery, roughly chopped
sugar, to taste

for the spice bag
1 piece of muslin
4 whole peppercorns
8 crushed pimento seeds
4 cloves
1 bunch of thyme
2 bay leaves

for the serving vegetables
2 carrots, peeled
1 sweet potato, peeled
2 green bananas, peeled
1 small pumpkin, quartered and skinned
1 christophene, peeled and halved

Take a large pan and immerse the beef in 1 litre/1¾ pints of cold water. Gently bring to the boil and skim away any scum that floats to the top.

Tie the herbs and spices up in the muslin and add to the pan with the roughly chopped vegetables and the sugar.

After the beef has simmered for 1 hour, pour off some cooking liquor into a separate pan, bring to the boil and add the serving vegetables individually, starting with the carrots then the sweet potato. After another 5 minutes add the green bananas, pumpkin and christophene. These will take no time at all to cook. When ready, remove the beef and keep warm. Discard the roughly chopped vegetables and the spice bag. Reduce the cooking liquid to make a sauce.

# for the barbie

Barbecues are absolutely fabulous. They conjure up that feel-good factor of the great outdoors: the sun shining, having a cool drink and chatting with friends . . . while a member of your family incinerates something that resembled food at one stage! I love all the barbecue recipes included in this chapter but my absolute favourite is barbecued jerk chicken and pineapple.

# barbecued jerk chicken and pineapple

The fresh pineapple used here really gives the dish that tangy edge which will have your guests talking about your barbecues for ever. Try to allow time for marinating before you start cooking.

serves 4

4 x 400–455g/14–16oz poussins
salt and freshly ground black pepper
3 tablespoons wet rub jerk seasoning (from a bottle)
2 tablespoons tomato ketchup
1 tablespoon honey
2 tablespoons chopped fresh coriander
2 tablespoons chopped fresh lemon balm
1 small pineapple, peeled and liquidized
3 tablespoons olive oil

Ask your butcher to spatchcock the poussins (removing the backbone). Season them with salt and pepper. Mix together the rest of the ingredients, add the poussins, and marinate for as long as possible before you start to cook.

Be sure to start the barbecuing really slowly, making sure the chicken cooks through properly and that the marinade does not caramelize and burn too soon.

# barbecued prawns with chermoula

This is a truly flavoursome dish. Chermoula is an ideal marinade for prawns, as its ingredients really complement fish. Pre-cooked prawns can be used, but raw prawns will give the best results. They need 2–4 hours marinating.

serves 4

1kg/2lb 3oz king prawns, in their shells

for the marinade
2 tablespoons finely chopped garlic
a pinch of ground cloves
1 teaspoon ground cumin
1 teaspoon ground coriander
½ teaspoon paprika
juice of 1 lime
2 handfuls of fresh coriander, chopped
olive oil

Wash and peel the prawns, removing the black line which runs down the back. Blend together all the marinade ingredients in a liquidizer, adding enough olive oil to create a smooth paste, and add the prawns. Leave for approximately 2–4 hours before cooking.

Barbecue the prawns over a moderate heat for 3–4 minutes per side, depending on their size.

Serve with black eye peas salsa (see page 173).

# charred lobster with garlic butter

This is oh-so-simple but completely moreish.

serves 4
**4 x 455g/1lb Scotch or Canadian lobsters**
**3 tablespoons extra virgin olive oil**
**½ garlic butter recipe (see page 187)**

Get the barbecue hot. Plunge the lobsters into boiling water for 2 minutes (this reduces shrinkage when cooking on the barbecue). Split the lobsters in half from head to tail and brush with olive oil. Place on the barbecue. Throw the claws on as well but leave the meat in the shell. Keep turning the lobster until the shell turns red, then remove from the heat. Baste the body with garlic butter. Remove the claws from the heat and crack them open. Toss the claws in garlic butter and serve with a pumpkin and apricot salad (see page 30).

# barbecued pork spare ribs

2kg/4½lb pork spare ribs
salt and freshly ground black pepper
2 tablespoons pimento oil (see page 189)
2 cloves of garlic, finely diced
1 red onion, finely diced
1 eating apple, peeled and diced
2 tablespoons jerk seasoning (see page 177, or from a bottle)
3 tablespoons tomato ketchup
1 tablespoon honey
285ml/½ pint pineapple juice

Get the barbecue hot. Lightly season the ribs. Heat the pimento
oil in a pan, add the garlic, onion and apple and cook over a low heat
for 3–4 minutes. Add the jerk seasoning, ketchup and honey and mix
well. Add the pineapple juice and mix again. Leave to simmer for
20 minutes. Season. When cool, coat the spare ribs with the mixture,
and place on the barbecue for 20–30 minutes, turning and basting
the ribs every 10 minutes. Remove when the ribs are crispy and
golden brown.

# chargrilled baby back rack

Baby back rack – spare ribs of pork. They need 4–8 hours marinating time.

serves 4
2 x 1.5–2kg/3½–4½lb baby back racks
juice of 1 lime

for the marinade
2 tablespoons honey
3 tablespoons tomato ketchup
2 tablespoons Dijon mustard
3 cloves of garlic
2 tablespoons crushed pimento seeds
juice of 1 lime
a splash of West Indian hot pepper sauce
salt and freshly ground black pepper

Blend all the marinade ingredients together in a food processor. Wash the racks in lime juice and water. Pat the meat dry and add to the marinade. Leave to marinate for 4–8 hours before use. When ready, place the meat on the hottest part of the barbecue to get a really good colouring and that unmistakable charcoal flavour. After 5–8 minutes move the racks to a cooler part of the barbecue and let the meat gently cook for a further 10–15 minutes.

Serve these delicious racks with baked sweet potatoes and tomato and onion salad (see page 32).

# grilled salmon and tuna kebabs

I prefer cooking these kebabs on my homemade brick barbecue. It's very simple to use and much safer than a portable barbecue. Tuna and salmon are a great kebab combination because their cooking times are more or less the same. You need to start the marinade 4–8 hours in advance.

serves 4

170g/6oz salmon, cut in cubes
170g/6oz tuna, cut in cubes
2 red peppers, cut in squares
2 yellow peppers, cut in squares
2 red onions, quartered
4 tomatoes, halved
4 mushrooms, halved

for the marinade

4 tablespoons sherry vinegar
2 tablespoons honey
4 tablespoons Pika pepper sauce (from a bottle)
juice of 1 lime
3 tablespoons extra virgin olive oil

Combine the marinade ingredients in a bowl, add the fish and vegetables and marinate for 4–8 hours before use.

Thread the fish and vegetables on to wet wooden skewers and brush with oil. Place on the hot barbecue, turning frequently. They will only take 4 or 5 minutes.

Serve with a lovely sweet potato salad (see page 28).

# jerk poussin

You will need to season the poussins a day before you intend to cook
them. They are fantastic cooked on the barbecue. Add some wood
chippings to the coals to give that authentic flavour, and if you can find
banana leaves, use these to cover the barbecue to create more smoke
and flavour.

serves 4

**4 poussins**
**6 tablespoons wet rub jerk seasoning (from a bottle)**
**salt and freshly ground black pepper**
**juice of 1 lime**

Split the poussins in half down the backbone. Wash well and pat
dry with kitchen paper. Apply the jerk seasoning and a little salt and
pepper and leave to marinate for 12–24 hours. When the barbecue is
ready, cook the poussins on the hottest part until they become charred.
This will take about 15–20 minutes. Then move them to a cooler area of
the barbecue, so the chicken continues cooking gently.

After another 20–25 minutes the birds will be ready to eat. Serve
with chargrilled corn on the cob.

# rice, pulses, noodles and grains

Rice, beans and peas are a staple part of the Caribbean diet. They are all very easy to prepare, and you can come up with many exciting dishes from the very best ingredients.

There are various types of rice – basmati is my favourite because of its natural perfume, which complements most types of cuisine. You can experiment with different flavours, with herbs, spices, or even different butters and stocks. As a wonderful nutritious source, rice has to be one of the most popular grains in the world.

Couscous is a delicious grain normally used in North African cooking, but it is not unsimilar to grains used in the Caribbean.

# rice and peas

There are many variations of this dish, as there are many types of peas and beans. I will use my particular favourite, which just happens to be the most popular in the Caribbean. This dish is a perfect accompaniment for chicken or can be served as a vegetarian dish in its own right.

serves 4

90g/3½oz dried red kidney beans, soaked overnight
255g/9oz basmati rice
55g/2oz coconut cream
1 bunch of fresh thyme, leaves picked
1 spring onion, chopped
2 cloves of garlic, chopped
1 pig's tail (optional)
1.8 litres/3 pints water
salt and freshly ground black pepper

Drain the soaked kidney beans and put in a pan with the water and all the ingredients except the rice.

Gently bring to the boil. Boil for 10 minutes, then turn down the heat and simmer for 45–60 minutes. Add the rice and cook for a further 20 minutes. During that time the rice should soak up all the remaining liquid. If it begins to boil dry, add a little more water.

Note: Allow the beans to cook in plenty of liquid. You may need to drain off a little liquid before adding the rice. You can always add a little water if you need to.

# seasoned rice

1 tablespoon coconut oil
1 small red onion, diced
1 clove of garlic, chopped
1 Scotch bonnet chilli, diced
½ a red pepper, diced
1 carrot, diced
310g/11oz basmati rice
salt and freshly ground black pepper
1–2 bay leaves
565ml/1 pint water or stock to cover rice

Heat the oil in a pan and cook all the vegetables until soft. Add the pre-washed rice to the pan and stir. Season, add the bay leaves, and cover with water or stock. Simmer for 10–15 minutes or until all the moisture is absorbed.

# tomato rice

This is a very simple dish which is full of flavour and has a wonderful colour.

serves 4

1 tablespoon olive oil
½ an onion, finely chopped
1 clove of garlic, finely chopped
2 spring onions, cut into chunks
310g/11oz basmati rice
1 level teaspoon garam masala
a sprinkling of saffron
3 tablespoons tomato fondue (see page 167)
565ml/1 pint vegetable stock
3 sun-dried tomatoes
salt and freshly ground black pepper
2 sprigs of fresh coriander, to garnish

Put the oil in a pan, and soften the onion, garlic and spring onions. Add the rice and cook for a further couple of minutes, then add the garam masala and saffron. Now add the tomato fondue and stock and leave to simmer until the rice has absorbed all the liquid.

When the rice has cooked, dice the confit tomatoes and add them to the rice. Season, and serve with fresh coriander.

# couscous

Couscous is a grain which is widely used in North African cooking.
With the addition of various ingredients it makes a wonderful
substitute for rice. It can be eaten hot or cold and is great as a salad.

serves 4

225g/8oz couscous
salt and freshly ground black pepper
2 dessertspoons olive oil
140ml/5fl oz stock or water
½ a yellow pepper, finely diced
½ a red pepper, finely diced
1 red onion, finely diced
8 fresh coriander leaves
1 lime

Place the couscous in a bowl and season. Add the olive oil and mix
well. Bring the stock or water to the boil and pour this over the
couscous – just enough to cover it. Stir and cover with clingfilm to let
it steam for a few minutes. Add the peppers, onion and coriander and
mix well. Finally, squeeze the lime juice over and serve.

# chickpeas

A lovely pulse but one not used very much in my household when I was growing up. Since becoming a chef, however, I have used chickpeas in various different recipes. They are simply delightful.

serves 4

255g/9oz dried chickpeas (or 2 x 400g/14oz tins, drained)
1 tablespoon coconut cream
1 clove of garlic, chopped
1 onion, sliced
a pinch of bicarbonate of soda
salt and freshly ground black pepper
extra virgin olive oil
lemon juice

for the spice bag
1 piece of muslin
4 black peppercorns, crushed
5 sprigs of fresh thyme
4 cumin seeds, crushed

If using dried chickpeas, soak them for 24 hours in cold water. Rinse and place in a pan. Cover with fresh water. Tie the spices up in the muslin. Add the coconut cream, garlic, onion, bicarbonate of soda and the spice bag and bring to the boil.

Now here is the tricky part – depending on the size of the chickpeas and their soaking time, the cooking time will vary anywhere between 1 and 1½ hours, so keep an eye on them. Don't let them boil dry. Only when the chickpeas are cooked should salt be added. If added before, the salt will harden the skin of the pulses.

To serve, stir a little extra virgin olive oil into the chickpeas. Finish with some black pepper and a squeeze of lemon juice.

# cornmeal à la crème

This dish can be served either with meat or fish, or on its own with some vegetables on the side.

serves 2

2 or 3 cloves of garlic, crushed
1 small onion, finely diced
olive oil
565ml/1 pint milk
140g/5oz cornmeal
55g/2oz Parmesan cheese (optional)
a pinch of grated nutmeg
115g/4oz butter
285ml/½ pint double cream
salt and freshly ground black pepper

Cook the garlic and onion in a little oil until translucent. Pour on the milk and bring to the boil. Add the cornmeal, stirring continuously. Add the Parmesan and nutmeg and stir until the mixture starts to thicken to your required texture. If it starts to thicken up too much, add a bit more milk. Stir in the butter and cream, season and serve.

# turned cornmeal

serves 4

2 tablespoons olive oil
1 small onion, chopped
1 spring onion, chopped
½ a red pepper, chopped
2 tomatoes, peeled, deseeded and chopped
6–8 okra, diced
1 clove of garlic, crushed
115g/4oz cornmeal
565ml/1 pint milk
55ml/2fl oz coconut milk
salt and freshly ground black pepper
1 teaspoon fresh thyme leaves

Heat the oil in a large pan and sauté the vegetables and garlic. Remove from the pan. Add the cornmeal to the pan and stir for about a minute.

Add half the milk and the coconut milk, and continue to cook until the mixture thickens.

Season, add the thyme, and adjust the consistency by adding more milk until you have the texture you want. Stir the vegetables back in.

Serve with fish or on its own as a vegetarian snack.

see page 103 boiled beef served with island vegetables

see page 90 curried shank of lamb with couscous

see page 97 | roast breast of duck with confit legs

pages 109, 110 barbecued pork spare ribs with chargrilled baby back rack

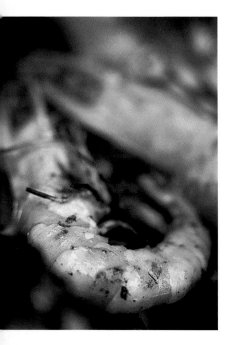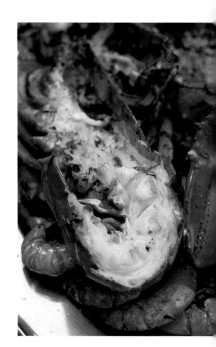

left barbecued prawns; right charred lobster with garlic butter

see page 114 rice and peas

# stir-fried egg noodles

I usually make this dish after I've had a big meal the day before, as I probably have bits and bobs to use up. For example, cooked meat, rice or vegetables. The addition of a few herbs, spices and egg noodles means that a marvellous dish can easily be created.

2 tablespoons vegetable oil
1 onion, finely diced
1 clove of garlic, finely chopped
1 Scotch bonnet chilli, finely diced
115g/4oz cooked meat or fish
2 spring onions, chopped
1 red pepper, diced
55g/2oz roasted corn kernels
55g/2oz peas
115g/4oz cooked rice
115g/4oz dried egg noodles
salt and freshly ground black pepper
1 tablespoon Chinese five-spice
1 teaspoon ground pimento seed
a handful of fresh coriander, chopped

Heat a little oil in a pan and cook the onion, garlic and Scotch bonnet over a low heat until soft. Add your meat or fish, spring onions, red pepper, corn kernels and peas. Then add the rice. Turn up the heat and stir-fry all the ingredients.

Blanch the egg noodles in hot water for 2 minutes, then drain and add to the stir-fry. Season well with salt, black pepper, five-spice and pimento seeds. Finish with plenty of chopped coriander.

# puddings and cakes

These puddings and cakes are not traditionally Caribbean but being self-indulgent, I'm including them here as they are my favourites.

I've kept the recipes simple so they can be followed easily. I have included a basic crumble with an apple and mango filling, a zabaglione Caribbean and, of course, chocolate brownies, which I totally adore.

# caramelized pineapple with tamarind ice cream

This is not a typical Caribbean dessert, but it's one which will complement any West Indian meal.

serves 4

4 egg yolks
280g/10oz caster sugar
285ml/½ pint milk
1 vanilla pod
115g/4oz tamarind purée
2 measures of rum
285ml/½ pint double cream
1 small fresh pineapple
225g/8oz butter
3 sprigs of fresh mint

To make the ice cream, whisk the yolks with half the sugar until double in volume. Boil the milk and add the vanilla pod. Whisk into the yolk mixture, return to a clean pan and put on a very low heat. Add the tamarind and rum. Add the cream and place in an ice-cream machine. Churn and leave to freeze.

Meanwhile, peel the pineapple, take out the hard core and slice into 3cm/1¼ inch thick pieces. Place the remaining sugar in a pan with the butter and cook until the mixture starts to caramelize, then add the pineapple. When the pineapple is nicely coated place in a serving bowl. Put a generous scoop of ice cream on the pineapple and garnish with mint.

# sweet banana fritters

makes 12 fritters
170g/6oz flour
85g/3 oz caster sugar
a pinch of salt
285ml/½ pint milk
15g/½oz fresh yeast
oil for deep-frying
2 bananas, peeled and sliced
65g/2¼oz icing sugar

Sieve the flour, sugar and salt into a bowl. Warm a little milk to body temperature, and dissolve the yeast. Add the yeast mixture to the flour. Add the rest of the milk and whisk until the batter is smooth. Preheat the oil to 160°C/315°F. Lightly dip the banana slices in the icing sugar, coat with the batter and place in the hot oil. When the fritters are golden brown, remove from the oil, dust with the remaining icing sugar, and serve.

These fritters can be served with ice-cream, a fruit purée or just fresh cream.

# fresh fruit platter and champagne sabayon

serves 4

8 strawberries, halved
1 paw-paw, peeled, deseeded and quartered
1 mango, peeled, deseeded and sliced
1 star fruit, sliced into 8 pieces
1 punnet of raspberries
1 Charentais melon, peeled, deseeded and quartered

for the sabayon

4 egg yolks
115g/4oz caster sugar
130ml/4½fl oz champagne
a pinch of grated nutmeg

Arrange the fruit on a plate.

Whisk the egg yolks and sugar together in a bowl until white. Add the champagne, set the bowl over a pan of boiling water, and whisk until doubled in volume. When finished add a pinch of nutmeg. Serve the fruit with the sabayon drizzled over.

# zabaglione caribbean

This is an absolutely moreish rich dessert of Italian origin. With the use of rum instead of marsala this becomes amazingly heartwarming, and believe me, after a tumbler of this you will think you are in the Caribbean!

serves 4–6
12 egg yolks
140g/5oz caster sugar
155ml/5½fl oz dark or white rum
1 tablespoon cocoa powder, sifted
115g/4oz good chocolate, grated

Mix the egg yolks and sugar in an electric mixer until the mixture has doubled in volume or has turned a rich white colour. Add the rum to the mixture and place in a bowl over a pan of hot water, continually whisking for 8–10 minutes, or until the mixture is really thick. (Do not let it get too hot or the eggs will scramble.)

To serve, pour into small tumblers. Dust with cocoa powder and sprinkle some fresh chocolate on top. Serve with coconut drops (see page 128) . . . delightful!

# coconut drops

makes 8–10 cakes
300g/10oz fresh coconut, shelled and diced (keep the juice)
5g/¼oz fresh ginger, finely diced
300g/10oz soft brown sugar
zest of 1 lime

Put the coconut in a pan with its juice and add enough water to cover. Add the ginger and gently simmer for 6–8 minutes. Add the brown sugar, and cook for 10–15 minutes or until the mixture has become syrupy and thick and is coating the coconut.

Add the lime zest and cook for 1 minute more. Spoon the mixture on to greaseproof paper. You can either spoon it in 8–10 round cakes, or you can pour all the mixture on to the greaseproof paper at once, smooth until flat, and when cool cut into fingers. I love to serve them with zabaglione Caribbean (see page 127).

# spiced rice pudding with raspberry compote

serves 4–6

565ml/1 pint milk
285ml/½ pint double cream
85g/3oz caster sugar
1 vanilla pod
½ a cinnamon stick
2 cloves
140g/5oz short-grain rice
110g/4oz butter
good pinch of grated nutmeg
1 tablespoon ground cinnamon

## for the raspberry compote

110g/4oz caster sugar
55ml/2fl oz water
110g/4oz frozen raspberries
140g/5oz fresh raspberries

To make the rice pudding, bring to the boil the milk, cream, sugar, vanilla pod, cinnamon stick and cloves. Remove from the heat. In another pan stir the rice grains in the butter with nutmeg and ground cinnamon until all the rice grains are coated in spices. At this stage start adding the infused milk. Once all the milk is added, leave to simmer for 45 minutes–1 hour. Finish by adding a little knob of butter.

To make the compote, put the sugar, water and frozen raspberries into a pan and heat gently. When the mixture has a syrupy consistency and has started to thicken, add the fresh raspberries. It's very easy to make and a lot better than jam! Serve the compote with the rice pudding.

# sweet potato pudding

serves 6–8

2 sweet potatoes, peeled and puréed
425ml/¾ pint milk
140ml/¼ pint coconut milk
1 teaspoon vanilla essence
¼ teaspoon ground cinnamon
¼ teaspoon grated nutmeg
2 eggs
zest of ½ a lemon
zest of ½ a lime
1 tart case, baked blind (see page 43)
2 teaspoons sugar

Preheat the oven to 180°C/350°F/gas 4. Place the puréed sweet potatoes into a bowl and put to one side. Gently warm the milk and coconut milk in a thick-bottomed pan, being careful not to let the mixture boil. Add the vanilla essence, ground cinnamon and nutmeg. Beat this mixture into the eggs with the lemon and lime zest. Add the sweet potato purée. Pour into the tart case and bake in the preheated oven for about 45 minutes. When it is almost ready, sprinkle the top with sugar and return it to the oven for a couple more minutes. This will give the tart a lovely glaze.

# sweet pastry

200g/7oz butter
90g/3½oz icing sugar
1 egg
400g/14oz plain flour
zest of 1 orange

Cream the butter and the icing sugar together. Add the egg and then slowly add the flour until the mixture forms a dough, adding a little water if necessary. Add the orange zest. Leave to rest for 1 hour.

When ready to use, flour a surface and roll out to 8cm/3 inches larger than the tin you are using.

# bread and butter pudding

serves 4–6

55g/2oz butter
10 slices of bread, crusts removed
zest and juice of 1 orange
a handful of sultanas, soaked in rum
565ml/1 pint milk
285ml/½ pint double cream
90g/3½oz caster sugar
a pinch of grated nutmeg
1 vanilla pod
8 eggs

Preheat the oven to 160°C/325°F/ gas 3. Butter the bread and cut into quarters. Arrange in a baking dish and sprinkle each piece with the orange zest and sultanas. Gently heat the milk, cream, sugar, orange juice, nutmeg and vanilla pod. Remove the pod after 5 minutes and scrape the seeds back into the milk and cream.

Whisk the eggs and pour the milk mixture on to them, whisking all the time. Strain over the sliced bread and gently bake in the preheated oven for approximately 30–40 minutes or until the custard is firm to the touch.

# basic crumble mixture

This crumble mix can be precooked on a baking sheet at
200°C/400°F/gas 6 until golden brown and then sprinkled on to your
chosen fruit filling, or just used from raw, and cooked for longer. Both
methods produce delicious results. Examples of favourite fruit fillings:
pear and plum; strawberry, paw-paw and apple; plum; peach and
pineapple.

400g/14oz plain flour
140g/5oz butter
200g/7oz caster sugar
a pinch of ground pimento seeds

Mix the flour and butter with your fingertips until well incorporated.
Add the sugar and pimento. Combine well.

# apple and mango crumble

Crumble has become embedded in Caribbean culture. Almost every family I know will create their own rendition of this classic, normally served with – wait for it – tinned or fresh custard, cream or ice-cream, or all of the above. Can't wait! This apple and mango filling is my absolute favourite.

serves 6–8

55g/2oz butter
455g/1lb Bramley cooking apples, cored, peeled and sliced into wedges
2–3 mangoes, peeled and cut into large slices
a pinch of ground cloves
a pinch of ground mixed spice
a pinch of freshly grated nutmeg
1 x basic crumble mix recipe, precooked (see page 133)

Preheat the oven to 190°C/375°F/gas 5. Melt the butter in a pan and gently toss the apples, mangoes and spices in it for about a minute until all the fruit is coated.

Place in a serving dish and top with a thin sprinkling of the crumble mix. Bake in the preheated oven for 10 minutes, until golden brown. If using the crumble mix from raw, cook for 15–20 minutes.

# chocolate brownies

Not a typical Caribbean recipe but one that I absolutely love.

makes 6–8
225g/8oz butter
140g/5oz cocoa powder
4 eggs
140g/5oz caster sugar
1 teaspoon vanilla essence
140g/5oz plain flour
90g/3½oz chopped hazelnuts

Preheat the oven to 180°C/350°F/gas 4. Butter a bread tin or a 20–25cm (8–10 inch) cake tin and line with greaseproof paper.

Melt the butter in a pan and mix in the cocoa powder. Whisk the eggs with the caster sugar and vanilla essence and add to the butter and cocoa mixture. Add all the other ingredients, mix well and pour into the cake tin.

Bake in the preheated oven for 15–20 minutes. Once cooked, remove from the oven. It is important that you leave the brownies to cool before turning out of the mould. They should be lovely and gooey in the middle. When cool, cut into squares.

Dust with icing sugar and serve with a raspberry sauce and vanilla ice-cream.

# chocolate pots

750ml/26fl oz milk
750ml/26fl oz cream
125g/4½oz sugar
3 egg yolks
455g/1lb best-quality dark chocolate

Preheat the oven to 160°C/325°F/gas 3. On a gentle heat, bring the milk and cream to the boil.

Whisk the sugar and egg yolks until white. Pour on the milk and cream and whisk.

Melt the chocolate in a glass bowl over some hot water. Add it to the egg mixture. Pour into ramekins and bake in the preheated oven for approximately 20–30 minutes. Add some rum to whipped cream and serve with the chocolate pots.

# rum and raisin cheesecake

This cheesecake is totally and utterly delicious – you must try it!

### for the filling
a handful of raisins
rum, to cover the raisins
400g/14oz cream cheese
3 eggs, beaten
565ml/1 pint double cream

### for the base
145g/5½ oz digestive biscuits
butter to bind

Lightly butter a 25cm/10 inch cake tin and line with greaseproof paper.
Crush the digestive biscuits in a mixer or with a rolling-pin. Melt the
butter and gradually add to the biscuit. Place the biscuit mixture in
the bottom of the cake tin and press until you have a firm and even
layer. Refrigerate.

Put the raisins in a small pan. Cover with rum and bring to the boil.
Leave to simmer for about 5 minutes until the raisins swell up.

Soften the cream cheese before use and place in a large bowl. Beat
until smooth. Add the eggs and raisins. Lightly whip the cream and
fold into the mixture. Preheat the oven to 180°C/350°F/gas 4. Pour the
cheese mixture on to the biscuit base and bake for about 45 minutes.
Leave to cool and serve with sweetened cream.

# rum cake

You will need to soak the fruit in the alcohol for 1–2 weeks prior to baking.

115g/4oz mixed fruit
115g/4oz sultanas
115g/4oz prunes
115g/4oz currants
white wine
rum
200g/7oz butter
200g/7oz margarine
200g/7oz soft dark brown sugar
10 whole eggs, beaten
200g/7oz plain flour
200g/7oz self-raising flour
1 tablespoon ground mixed spice
1 tablespoon vanilla essence
2–3 tablespoons gravy browning

Put all the dried fruit in a bowl and pour on enough rum and wine in equal quantities to cover. Leave for 1–2 weeks before making the cake. When you are ready to cook, put the fruit and soaking liquid into a liquidizer and blitz to a smooth paste.

Cream the butter and the margarine with the sugar, until soft. Gradually add the eggs. Add the liquidized fruit, and fold in the sieved flours. Add the mixed spice and vanilla essence. Mix in gravy browning as necessary to give the cake that dark rich look.

Preheat the oven to 180°C/350°F/gas 4. Grease a 25cm/10 inch cake tin and line with greaseproof paper. Pour in the mixture and bake the cake for approximately 1 hour or until cooked. Check the cake by inserting a paring knife or skewer into the centre. If it comes out clean the cake is ready; if not, leave to cook a while longer.

When the cake is ready, leave to cool. Then make little holes in the top using a skewer and pour 155ml/5½fl oz of rum over the top of the cake, or more depending on how strong you like it.

Leave for 2 days before eating.

Don't eat and drive!

# banana cake

115g/4oz butter
400g/14oz soft brown sugar
2 eggs
6 bananas, crushed with a fork
115g/4oz raisins
680g/1½lb self-raising flour
1 teaspoon grated nutmeg
1 teaspoon ground mixed spice
½ teaspoon salt
285ml/½ pint milk
2½ teaspoons vanilla essence

Cream the butter and sugar and beat in the eggs. Add the bananas. Sift in the flour, salt, nutmeg and mixed spice. Stir well.

Add the milk, vanilla essence and raisins. Mix together well. If the mixture becomes too stiff, add more milk, a little at a time.

Preheat the oven to 180°C/350°F/gas 4. Grease a 20cm/8 inch cake tin and line with greaseproof paper. Bake in the preheated oven for 1 hour, until done.

# drinks

Beverages play a huge role in many countries, but in the West Indies, being a hot country, drinks are very important.

Using fresh fruit and vegetables, all types of non-alcoholic concoctions can be conjured up. The Caribbean also boasts an abundance of quality rums and each island has its own brand, which differs from the rest in strength, colour and flavour. Every island, of course, thinks that theirs is the best.

Herbal drinks are also quite popular, and everybody has their own special remedy for everyday aches and pains. There are many wild herbs in the West Indies, which can be used to make infusions for medicinal purposes. My grandfather has an amazing knowledge of the different herbs and roots which can be used in cooking.

Some drinks are used as digestifs, some drinks just to quench thirst. Regardless, I hope you have great fun making and tasting these mouth-watering drinks.

# sky juice

This drink has a fascinating name, but it is basically a Caribbean slush puppie. Any flavour of syrup can be poured over shaved ice to create this refreshing drink. I particularly like to use pineapple-flavoured syrup. Syrups are easily available from most supermarkets and ethnic food stores.

serves 1

140ml/¼ pint syrup, chosen flavour
lots of shaved ice

Put the shaved ice into a chilled glass and pour the syrup over the top.

# carrot juice

This is a very basic recipe – the only ingredient is carrots. If you use organic carrots you will get fantastic-tasting juice.

serves 4

**10 large organic carrots**

Top and tail the carrots. Wash, peel and put into the juicer. Serve chilled or with lots of crushed ice. As a variation, add the zest and juice of 4 limes.

# carrot juice punch

This punch is very thirst-quenching and is usually served every Sunday at home with lunch. Nurishment is a tinned supplement drink which you should be able to find at any supermarket.

serves 4

5 large carrots, washed and peeled
215ml/7½fl oz Guinness
1 can of Nurishment
½ teaspoon grated nutmeg
1 teaspoon vanilla essence
3 tablespoons condensed milk (optional)

Put the carrots into a juicer and then mix the juice with the rest of the ingredients. Serve chilled or with lots of crushed ice.

see page 137   rum and raisin cheesecake

see page 124 caramelized pineapple with tamarind ice cream

see page 126 fresh fruit platter and champagne sabayon

see page 129

spiced rice pudding with raspberry compote

see page 135  chocolate brownies

from left to right sky juice, cucumber juice and mint, carrot juice

see pages 172,
171, 176, 173
clockwise from top left pepper frenzy salsa; chargrilled sweet corn and tomato salsa; pink grapefruit, orange and tomato salsa; black eye peas salsa

# rum punch

juice of 2 limes
juice of 3 oranges
juice of 1 pineapple
3 double shots of white rum
1 double shot of dark rum
mixed fruit
crushed ice
strawberry syrup

Mix the fruit juices and rums and chill.
Dice the fruit and add to the punch so it can soak up the flavour.
Finish with crushed ice and a splash of strawberry syrup.

# guinness punch

serves 4
240ml/8½fl oz Guinness
½ a can of Nurishment (see page 144)
115ml/4fl oz milk
½ teaspoon grated nutmeg
2 teaspoons vanilla essence
3 tablespoons condensed milk (optional)

Pour the Guinness into a bowl. Add the milk and Nurishment. Sprinkle the nutmeg over to taste, and add the vanilla essence. If you want to make the drink sweeter, add the condensed milk. Chill before serving, or serve over crushed ice.

# planters' punch

serves 2

4 shots of dark rum
8 shots of orange juice
juice of 1 lime
2 shots of grenadine
sugar (optional)
crushed ice to serve

Mix and pour over crushed ice.

# patrick's punch

serves 2
285ml/½ pint fresh orange juice
285ml/½ pint carrot juice
juice of ½ a lime
4 tablespoons strawberry purée

Combine the juices and spoon the purée over the top.

# peanut punch

serves 2

115g/4oz roasted peanuts
565ml/1 pint soya milk
½ teaspoon vanilla essence
½ teaspoon ground cinnamon
ice to serve

Blend the peanuts, soya or coconut milk, vanilla and cinnamon in a blender until the mixture is smooth. Sweeten to taste and serve well chilled with ice.

# guava, mango and orange punch

serves 2

140ml/¼ pint guava juice, bottled
140ml/¼ pint fresh mango juice
285ml/½ pint fresh orange juice
a squeeze of lime juice

Combine the juices, add the lime juice and mix well.

# mango drink

serves 2–4
8 ripe mangoes, peeled, deseeded and chopped
55ml/2fl oz lime juice
255ml/9fl oz water
255ml/9fl oz rosewater
crushed ice

Blend the mangoes, lime juice and water until smooth. Stir in the rosewater. Strain and serve with lots of crushed ice.

# pumpkin drink

serves 2

225g/8oz pumpkin, steamed and cubed
565ml/1 pint milk
¼ teaspoon grated nutmeg
¼ teaspoon ground cinnamon
½ teaspoon vanilla essence
honey or sugar to taste
ice to serve

Mash the pumpkin and combine with the milk. Strain the mixture, dilute if necessary and add the nutmeg, cinnamon and vanilla. Sweeten with honey or sugar and serve well chilled with ice.

# cerassie tea

This tea can be taken as a tonic and was forced upon me as a child.
The taste is quite ghastly if not sweetened with honey. This wild herb
grows by the river in the Caribbean, and its appearance is very similar
to thyme, although that is where similarities end! You can buy cerassie
in teabag form now, but normally it would be made like this.

makes a big pot
**1 large bunch of cerassie, washed**
**water to cover**
**2 tablespoons honey (optional)**

Place the cerassie in a large pan. Cover with water and bring to the
boil. Simmer for 10–15 minutes or until the tea is the required strength.
Leave to steep.

Strain off the tea and serve, sweetened with honey to taste.

# lemon grass tea

I've got a little story about this tea! I was first introduced to it as a child when visiting Jamaica. I had been at the beach with my grandad and on the way back to the house he was nimbly running from one side of the road to the other pulling what I thought were weeds out of the ground, when I asked what he was doing. He lectured me about the life and times of lemon grass!

This tea is a real stress-reliever and has a great aroma which is really moreish. It also has healing properties to combat flu and colds. It can be bought in teabag form from most health food shops and all major supermarkets.

makes a big pot
**1 large bunch of lemon grass**
**water to cover**
**2 tablespoons honey**

Put the lemon grass in a large pan. Cover with water and bring to the boil. Simmer for 10–15 minutes until the tea is the required strength. Leave to steep. Strain off the tea and serve, sweetened with honey to taste.

# cucumber juice and mint

This is an extremely refreshing beverage, which also has medicinal properties. Cucumber juice is good for chronic constipation and it can also be used as a coolant for skin sores and burns.

serves 2–4
**6 cucumbers, peeled and deseeded**
**6 fresh mint leaves**
**crushed ice**
**a pinch of celery salt**

Put the cucumbers through a juicer.

Chop the mint, saving 2–3 leaves for garnish. Add the chopped mint to the cucumber juice.

Pour on to the crushed ice and leave to stand for 10 minutes. Serve with celery salt.

# stocks, sauces, salsas and dressings

I really deliberated about this chapter. Most of the well-known Caribbean dishes are either one-pot dishes, as in stews where water rather than stock is added and the natural flavours of the ingredients do the rest, or barbecue dishes where sauces are made from natural juices or come out of a bottle.

Then I thought about fish dishes and salads. Although fresh fish is beautiful and sometimes needs only a squeeze of lemon or lime, depending on the method of cooking used, you might sometimes need a little court-bouillon or dressing. And no Caribbean cookbook could be complete without the addition of fresh Thousand Island dressing. After tasting my recipe you'll want to throw out that stuff you keep in the fridge!

# vegetable stock

2 carrots, chopped
1 leek, sliced
4 sticks of celery, sliced
1 onion, chopped
6 tomatoes, chopped
1 tablespoon olive oil

for the spice bag
a piece of muslin
4 pimento seeds, crushed
½ a head of garlic, cloves separated
fresh parsley stalks
1 bay leaf
2 sprigs of fresh thyme

Tie all the spice bag ingredients up in the muslin. Put all the vegetables into a saucepan with the olive oil and cook them gently without colouring. Add water to just cover and bring to the boil. Add the spice bag. Simmer for 30–45 minutes, skimming continually. Pass the liquid through a sieve and your vegetable stock is ready to use. You can also keep it refrigerated to use later.

# fish stock

2 white onions, sliced
1 large leek, sliced
bay leaves
fresh parsley stalks
2 tablespoons olive oil
1.4kg/3lb white fish bones
8 white peppercorns
3 slices of lemon

Put the vegetables and herbs into a large pan with the olive oil and cook gently without colouring. Add the well-washed fish bones and continue to cook for another 2 or 3 minutes. Pour water into the pan until the vegetables and bones are only just covered. Add the peppercorns and bring to the boil. Skim and simmer until you have a good strong flavour – it should take about 20 minutes. Add the lemon slices, leave to stand for about 8 minutes, and strain.

# shellfish stock

2 tablespoons olive oil
2kg/4½lb lobster or crab shells, crushed
1 large carrot, roughly chopped
1 large onion, roughly chopped
½ a bulb of fennel, sliced
1 bulb of garlic, halved
3–4 tomatoes, chopped
fresh tarragon
fresh chervil stalks
2 star anise

Heat the oil in a thick-bottomed pan and cook the shells gently until they colour lightly. Remove from the pan, add the vegetables, herbs and spices and cook for a couple of minutes. Put the shells back into the pan and stir. Add water to cover the ingredients, bring to the boil and skim. Simmer for 30–45 minutes, then strain and cool. This stock can be used immediately or refrigerated for use later.

# court-bouillon

This cooking liquor can be used for poaching fish or shellfish. It's a basic recipe, but different herbs and spices can be added to it to take the flavour in different directions, so experiment.

2 litres/3½ pints water
285ml/½ pint vinegar
2 sticks of celery, roughly chopped
½ an onion, roughly chopped
1 bulb of fennel, roughly chopped
1 large carrot, roughly chopped
6 white peppercorns
fresh parsley stalks
fresh thyme leaves
a pinch of salt

Put the water and vinegar in a pan. Add the vegetables, peppercorns, herbs and salt. Bring to the boil and leave to simmer. The court-bouillon can be refrigerated and used the next day.

# ackee rouille

3 egg yolks
2 red peppers
1 clove of garlic
115g/4oz tinned ackee
olive oil
a pinch of salt
a pinch of cayenne

Put the egg yolks in a liquidizer with the red peppers, garlic and half the ackee. Blend until smooth. Gradually add olive oil until you have a mayonnaise consistency. Season, fold in the remaining ackee and serve.

# mornay sauce

115g/4oz butter
115g/4oz flour
1 litre/1¾ pints warm milk
1 onion
5 or 6 cloves
2 bay leaves
150g/5½oz Cheddar cheese, grated
salt and freshly ground black pepper
a pinch of grated nutmeg

Melt the butter in a pan and add the flour, stirring well. Continue to cook but do not let the mixture colour. Gradually add the warm milk, stirring continuously. Stud the onion with the cloves and bay leaves. Add the studded onion to the pan and continue to cook for about 15 minutes. Then add the cheese, season and add the nutmeg for a wonderful pungent flavour.

# plantain and pumpkin sauce

This sauce is delicious with fish or vegetable dishes.

115ml/4fl oz olive oil
1 clove of garlic, crushed
1 small onion, diced
1 Scotch bonnet chilli, diced
2 tablespoons crushed coriander seeds
salt and freshly ground black pepper
2 ripe plantains, peeled and diced
170g/6oz ripe pumpkin or squash, peeled and diced
1.2 litres/2 pints stock
285ml/½ pint cream
zest of 1 lime

Put the olive oil in a thick-bottomed pan, and gently heat. Add the garlic, onion, Scotch bonnet and coriander seeds. Cook the ingredients for about 1 minute, seasoning lightly. Add the plantain and pumpkin and continue to cook for a further minute, then add the stock and cook until the pumpkin is soft.

Put all the ingredients into a liquidizer and purée. Pour the mixture into a sieve over a clean pan, add the cream and bring to the boil. Stir in the lime zest and correct the seasoning.

# barbecue sauce

140ml/¼ pint tomato ketchup
2 tablespoons mustard
1 tablespoon ground pimento seeds
2 teaspoons chopped fresh ginger
1 clove of garlic, chopped
½ a red pepper, deseeded and diced
1 Scotch bonnet chilli, diced
½ a red onion, diced
chopped fresh coriander

Mix all the ingredients together and serve.

# marinating barbecue sauce

140ml/¼ pint tomato ketchup
2 tablespoons mustard
2 tablespoons ground pimento seeds
1 heaped tablespoon ground ginger
2 cloves of garlic, finely chopped
2 tablespoons honey
½ teaspoon ground cloves
1 dessertspoon balsamic vinegar
½ a small pineapple, peeled and puréed

Mix all the ingredients together and use as a marinade for meat or fish
to be cooked on the barbecue.

# tomato fondue

4 tablespoons olive oil
1 red onion, finely diced
3 cloves of garlic, finely diced
2 tablespoons fresh thyme leaves
1 tablespoon tomato purée
2 x 400g/14oz tins of tomatoes, drained, deseeded and chopped
salt and freshly ground black pepper

Put the olive oil in a pan, add the red onion, garlic and thyme, and cook until soft. Add the tomato purée, and cook for 5 minutes. Add the tomatoes and continue to cook until there is no liquid left. Remove from the heat and leave to cool. The fondue can be refrigerated for 1 week.

# sweet potato salsa

This salsa is very easy to make but would grace any table.

2 large sweet potatoes
2 spring onions
1 Scotch bonnet chilli
2 tomatoes
1 cucumber
1 clove of garlic, crushed
1 small bunch of fresh parsley, roughly chopped
salt and freshly ground black pepper
ground pimento seeds
2 tablespoons white wine vinegar
4 tablespoons olive oil

Preheat the oven to 190°C/375°F/gas 5. Wash the sweet potatoes. Prick them and wrap them in foil. Bake in the preheated oven for about 20 minutes, making sure they do not get too soft. Leave to cool. Dice the spring onions and Scotch bonnet. Deseed and skin the tomatoes. Peel and dice the cucumber. Put all the vegetables in a bowl and mix together.

Add a little salt, pepper and ground pimento. Put the vinegar in a separate bowl and add the olive oil, whisking continuously until the two liquids emulsify.

Add the dressing to the vegetables and leave for 15 minutes before serving.

# tomato salsa

The wonderful thing about this dish is that the natural juices create their own sauce. I normally finish mine with a drizzle of olive oil. But members of my family like to use the world-famous Pika pepper sauce.

    4 tomatoes
    2 cloves of garlic, crushed
    salt and freshly ground black pepper
    ½ a red onion
    1 spring onion
    1 small bunch of fresh coriander
    3 tablespoons olive oil

Cut the tomatoes into quite large dice. Place in a bowl with any excess juice. Chop the garlic with some salt until it becomes a purée. Finely dice the red onion and spring onion. Roughly chop the coriander.
  Mix all the ingredients together and add the oil and seasoning.

# sun-dried tomato salsa

6 tomatoes
sea salt and freshly ground black pepper
2 cloves of garlic
1 teaspoon fresh thyme leaves
palm oil
2 spring onions
3 good pinches of saffron
zest and juice of 1 lime
1 small bunch of fresh parsley, roughly chopped

Wash the tomatoes and halve lengthways. Place them on a baking tray and sprinkle with salt and pepper.

Peel and thinly slice the garlic and place on top of the tomatoes. Sprinkle half the thyme leaves over the tomatoes, drizzle with a little palm oil and put in a very low oven (140°C/275°F/gas 1) for 3–4 hours. The tomatoes should not be completely dried.

Chop the spring onions and place in a frying-pan with the remaining thyme leaves, saffron and lime zest. Add a little palm oil and leave to cook for approximately 30 seconds or until all the colour has come out of the saffron.

Cut the tomatoes into large dice and add to the cooked ingredients. Squeeze the lime juice over the dish, and a drizzle of palm oil. Decorate with the chopped parsley.

# chargrilled sweet corn and tomato salsa

1 corn cob
140ml/¼ pint pimento oil (see page 189)
1 red pepper
1 avocado
2 Scotch bonnet chillies, chopped
2 plum tomatoes, chopped
1 small bunch of parsley
1 small bunch of fresh coriander
1 lime
140ml/¼ pint palm oil
salt and freshly ground black pepper

Normally corn can be put straight on to chargrill, but for this recipe
I like to blanch it by quickly plunging the ears into boiling water for
approximately 30–45 seconds first. Once blanched, brush the corn with
pimento oil and lightly chargrill on all sides. Carefully remove all the
kernels and place in a bowl.

Prick and chargrill the red pepper. Place in a bowl covered with
clingfilm for 5–10 minutes, then remove from the bowl and peel. Dice
the pepper flesh and add to the corn. Peel and dice the avocado, and
add to the bowl with the chillies and tomatoes.

Chop the parsley and coriander quite coarsely. Squeeze the lime
juice into a separate bowl and stir in the palm oil and pimento oil. Add
the fresh herbs and pour this dressing over the other ingredients.
Season and serve.

# pepper frenzy salsa

This salsa is particularly good with fried fish.

2 red peppers, diced
2 yellow peppers, diced
1 red chilli, diced
1 Scotch bonnet chilli, diced
2 spring onions, diced
1 clove of garlic, chopped
4 tomatoes, diced
pimento oil
1 small bunch of fresh coriander, chopped
1 small bunch of fresh mint, chopped
1 tablespoon tomato fondue (see page 167)
salt and freshly ground black pepper
olive oil

Quickly cook all the vegetables in the pimento oil, adding the tomatoes
last. Leave to cool, then stir in the herbs and tomato fondue and season
to taste. Add a drizzle of olive oil and serve.

# black eye peas salsa

255g/9oz black eye peas, soaked overnight
2 spring onions
2 sprigs of fresh thyme
2 cloves of garlic, chopped
1 Scotch bonnet chilli (optional)
90g/3½oz coconut cream
1 cinnamon stick
½ a cucumber
1 yellow pepper
2 tomatoes
salt and freshly ground black pepper
olive oil
chopped fresh parsley
juice of 1 lemon

Put the soaked peas in a large pan with twice their volume of water,
the spring onions, thyme, garlic, Scotch bonnet, coconut cream and
cinnamon stick. Simmer for 15–20 minutes or until the peas are soft.
When cooked, drain and leave to cool, reserving the cooking liquid.

Dice all the vegetables and mix with the peas. Add about 140ml/
¼ pint of the saved cooking liquid and season. Stir in some olive oil and
add the chopped parsley and lemon juice.

# aubergine salsa

4 aubergines
chopped fresh thyme
2 cloves of garlic, chopped
90g/3½oz rock salt
140ml/¼ pint olive oil
2 onions, chopped
1 Scotch bonnet chilli, diced
1 teaspoon paprika
1 teaspoon turmeric
4 tomatoes, peeled and chopped
1 cucumber, diced
zest and juice of 2 lemons
1 small bunch of fresh coriander

Cut the aubergines in half lengthways. Sprinkle each half with chopped thyme, garlic and rock salt (which will help draw out that bitter taste) and leave for 10 minutes.

Preheat the oven to 170°C/325°F/gas 3. Wrap each aubergine half in foil and bake in the preheated oven for approximately 10–15 minutes. Remove from the oven and roughly chop the aubergine flesh. Gently heat some olive oil in a pan and add the onions, Scotch bonnet, paprika and turmeric. Cook for about 30 seconds, then add the aubergine flesh.

Remove the pan from the heat and leave to cool, then add the tomatoes, cucumber, lemon juice and zest, and remaining olive oil. Stir in the chopped coriander and serve.

# fresh crab and mango salsa

This is a simple but sensational salsa to serve with fish or salad.
To make ginger vinegar, just steep some slices of root ginger in wine vinegar.

Try not to eat it all before your guests arrive – it is delicious!

2 ripe mangoes, peeled and deseeded
zest and juice of 1 lime
1 shallot, chopped
1 red chilli, chopped
2 tablespoons ginger vinegar
140g/5oz white crabmeat
1 small bunch of fresh coriander

Dice the mango flesh and put in a bowl. Add the lime juice and zest, shallot, red chilli and a splash of ginger vinegar. Put the crabmeat into a bowl, checking for shells.

Coarsely chop the coriander and add to the mango mixture. Sprinkle the crab over the mango and stir.

# pink grapefruit, orange and tomato salsa

2 pink grapefruits
2 oranges
2 tomatoes, peeled, deseeded and cut into strips
6 sprigs of fresh mint, chopped
70ml/2½fl oz pimento oil (see page 189)

Segment 1 grapefruit and 1 orange and squeeze the juice from the remaining fruit. Add the tomatoes. Whisk the pimento oil into the grapefruit and orange juice, add the fruit, chopped mint and serve.

# pat's jerk seasoning

1 bunch of thyme, leaves picked
2 cinnamon sticks, crushed
2 tablespoons chopped fresh coriander
1 teaspoon coriander seeds, crushed
2 tablespoons black peppercorns, crushed
1 teaspoon freshly grated nutmeg
3 teaspoons pimento seeds, crushed
6 cloves of garlic
4 Scotch bonnet chillies, seeds removed
2 teaspoons chopped fresh ginger
zest of 1 lime
juice of 2 limes
140ml/¼ pint olive oil

Combine all the ingredients in a liquidizer and blend until you have a smooth paste. It keeps for about 2 weeks in the refrigerator.

# fresh mango chutney

This is another of my favourite dishes, simply because it is so easy to make, and of course it's absolutely delicious with fish or meat.

½ teaspoon diced red onion
2 teaspoons chopped fresh ginger
½ teaspoon diced Scotch bonnet chilli
a pinch of freshly grated nutmeg
a pinch of ground cinnamon
2 tablespoons olive oil
2 dessertspoons brown sugar
2 dessertspoons sherry vinegar
juice of 2 limes
2 spring onions, chopped
2 large mangoes, peeled, deseeded and diced
4 teaspoons chopped fresh coriander

In a heavy-bottomed pan, soften the red onion, ginger, Scotch bonnet, nutmeg and cinnamon in the oil. When the pan is really sizzling, add the sugar, which will start to caramelize. Now add the sherry vinegar and the lime juice, and remove from the heat. Allow the mixture to cool, then add the spring onions and mangoes. Top with chopped coriander, and serve hot or cold.

# mayonnaise

3 egg yolks
3 teaspoons white wine vinegar
¼ teaspoon Dijon mustard
a splash of Tabasco or Worcestershire sauce
salt and freshly ground black pepper
285ml/½ pint vegetable oil

Put the egg yolks, vinegar, mustard and Tabasco or Worcestershire in a large metal bowl and whisk until the mixture doubles in volume. Add seasoning, then add the oil gradually, whisking continuously. Put your mayonnaise into a clean container and refrigerate.

# thousand island dressing

This is a variant of mayonnaise, with extra ingredients added.

1 x mayonnaise recipe (see page 179), using 1 extra egg yolk
1–2 tablespoons tomato ketchup
1 dessertspoon diced green pepper
1 dessertspoon diced red pepper
1 teaspoon diced red Scotch bonnet chilli
1 dessertspoon diced red onion
chopped fresh parsley and coriander

Make the mayonnaise and add all the other ingredients.

# marie rose dressing

This is another variation on mayonnaise.

1 x mayonnaise recipe (see page 179), using 1 extra egg yolk
1–2 tablespoons tomato ketchup
2 plum tomatoes, peeled, deseeded and diced
1 shot of brandy

Make the mayonnaise and add the other ingredients.

# orange and pink grapefruit dressing

3 oranges
2 pink grapefruits
1 tablespoon coriander seeds
285ml/½ pint olive oil
2 tablespoons chopped fresh coriander

Peel and segment 2 oranges and 1 grapefruit and dice. Juice the remaining orange and grapefruit. Place the coriander seeds in a frying-pan and heat gently until the seeds start to pop. Put the seeds into a grinder and blend to a powder.

Mix the olive oil, fruit juice and ground coriander seeds to make a dressing, and stir in the chopped coriander and diced fruit at the end. Leave to stand for an hour before serving.

# cherry tomato dressing

This dressing should be made 24 hours before you want to use it.

1 small bunch of fresh basil, chopped
455g/1lb cherry tomatoes, chopped
1 small red onion, chopped
1 clove of garlic, chopped
zest of 1 lime and 1 orange
3 sprigs of fresh thyme, leaves picked
3 tablespoons olive oil
1 tablespoon balsamic vinegar
rock salt and freshly ground black pepper

Put all the ingredients into a bowl and leave in the refrigerator to marinate overnight.

Next day, pour everything into a liquidizer and blend until the mixture is smooth. Adjust the seasoning if necessary and serve.

# balsamic dressing

This is a very simple but delicious dressing; good for serving with salads or with cold meats, poultry or fish.

2 shallots, finely diced
1 clove of garlic
3 tablespoons arachide or vegetable oil
3 tablespoons olive oil
2 tablespoons balsamic vinegar
salt and freshly ground black pepper

Put the shallots in a bowl. Crush the garlic with a little salt and add to the shallots.

Mix both the oils together. Pour the vinegar on to the shallots and garlic and then gradually incorporate the oils until you have achieved the required taste. Add salt and pepper, and serve.

# sweet curry vinaigrette

3 tablespoons pimento oil (see page 189)
2 tablespoons finely diced carrot
1 tablespoon finely diced onion
2 tablespoons curry powder
a pinch of saffron
1 wineglass of Sauternes
55ml/2fl oz olive oil
1 apple, cored, peeled and finely diced
2 tablespoons finely chopped fresh chives

Heat the pimento oil in a pan and soften the carrot and onion for 2–3 minutes. Add the curry powder and saffron and cook for a further minute.

Add the wine and simmer until reduced by half. Strain, discarding the vegetables. Add the olive oil to the remaining liquid, and stir in the diced apple and chopped chives.

# jerk butter

This is a beautiful way to finish a dish – really handy to have ready in your refrigerator.

255g/9oz unsalted butter
3 tablespoons jerk seasoning (see page 177, or bottled)
1 Scotch bonnet chilli, diced
1 small red onion, diced
2 tablespoons chopped fresh coriander
1 tablespoon chopped fresh parsley
zest and juice of 1 lime

Soften the butter and add all the other ingredients. Mix well, then roll up in clingfilm or greaseproof paper and refrigerate.

# garlic butter

255g/9oz unsalted butter
6 cloves of garlic, finely chopped
2 tablespoons finely chopped spring onion
juice of 1 lemon

Soften the butter and add all the other ingredients. Mix well, then roll
up in clingfilm or greaseproof paper and refrigerate.

# chilli and coconut butter

Serve this with meat or fish.

255g/9oz unsalted butter
2 Scotch bonnet chillies, finely diced
3 tablespoons coconut milk
2 tablespoons chopped fresh coriander
1 tablespoon grated fresh coconut
zest and juice of 1 lime

Soften the butter and add all the other ingredients. Mix well, then wrap in clingfilm or greaseproof paper and refrigerate.

# pimento oil

225g/8oz pimento seeds
a good pinch of saffron
400ml/14fl oz olive oil
2 cloves of garlic, crushed

Crush the pimento seeds in a pestle and mortar. Heat a frying-pan and dry fry the seeds gently for 1 minute. Add the saffron and fry for a few seconds, then add the olive oil and garlic. Gently simmer for 1 minute, then pour into a preserving jar and leave to cool.

Refrigerate once cool – it will keep a long time.

# curry oil

This should be made 24 hours before using.

285ml/½ pint olive oil
½ a shallot, chopped
½ a Scotch bonnet chilli, chopped
½ a clove of garlic, sliced
1 tablespoon curry powder
4 pimento seeds, crushed
4 black peppercorns, crushed
a pinch of saffron

Gently warm a thick-bottomed pan on the stove and add a little olive oil. Gently fry the shallot. When translucent add all the other ingredients and fry gently for a minute or so to cook the curry powder.
Add the rest of the oil to the pan and heat gently until it reaches body temperature. The oil should then be bottled and left to infuse.

# curry paste

Of course there are all sorts of wonderful curry powders and curry pastes on the market, and not very many people actually have the time to make their own. Basically this recipe is a combination of my favourite herbs and spices.

1 teaspoon cumin seeds
1 teaspoon coriander seeds
½ teaspoon mustard seeds
2 teaspoons pimento seeds
1 teaspoon black peppercorns
1 stick of cinnamon
a pinch of ground cloves
a pinch of grated nutmeg
1 teaspoon saffron
1 Scotch bonnet chilli, chopped
1 teaspoon chopped fresh ginger

Crush the cumin, coriander and mustard seeds, allspice berries, peppercorns and cinnamon in a pestle and mortar or a blender and add the other ingredients.

# glossary

**ackee** A well-known fruit from the Caribbean, originating from West Africa. It is red in colour, with shiny black seeds, and is delicate in flavour. Ackee is difficult to find fresh in Britain, but can be easily purchased tinned from Caribbean, Indian and other speciality food shops.

**aubergine** Also known as eggplant, originating from India, widely available in purple and white varieties. It has a very distinct flavour and the oldest and largest fruits contain the most seeds.

**baby back rack** The spare ribs of pork.

**balsamic** Matured sweet vinegar.

**basil** An aromatic herb, originating in India, giving a strong flavour of lemon and jasmine.

**butternut squash** This vegetable is related to the pumpkin family, the pulp usually being orange.

**callaloo** A green vegetable a bit like spinach. It is a staple food of many West Indians and can be bought tinned in Britain. Sometimes available fresh but does not have quite the same flavour as when grown in the Caribbean.

**cayenne** A form of pepper, strong and rather sharp in flavour. Originally grown in South America, it can now be found in France also. Cayenne is widely available all year round.

**cerassie** Known in the Caribbean as 'bush tea', this quite pungent herb is mainly used as tea, supposedly having medicinal properties.

**chermoula** A combination of spices, normally used in North African countries.

**chillies** There are so many different chilli varieties available, in red, green, yellow, orange and black form. The seeds especially and the flesh are extremely hot and should be used sparingly. Always remember to wash your hands well after handling chillies and not to touch the eyes (or any other sensitive areas). The juice can remain on the hands for hours. See also separate entry for Scotch bonnet.

**chives** Related to the spring onion, chives are the smallest and mildest member of the family and are widely used in Caribbean cooking. The familiar chives grown outdoors most closely resemble the flavour of those used in the Caribbean.

**christophene** Also known as cho-cho, coyote or choyote. This is a typical squash, originating from Mexico. The range available varies from green to white, and the prickly skin is removed before cooking. This vegetable will take on the flavour of the dish it is being used in.

**cho-cho** See Christophene.

**cinnamon** A spice obtained from Sri Lanka and China. It gives off a wonderful sweet aroma which can be quite penetrating, and has a hot spicy flavour.

**cloves** Well known for their medicinal as well as their culinary properties, cloves originated in the Moluccas and are often combined with cinnamon.

**coriander** This aromatic plant, also known as Chinese parsley, is grown for its seeds but mostly for its leaves, which are widely available.

**corn, Cornmeal** A cereal rich in starch and extensively used in the Caribbean and Europe. It can be used in soups, cakes or as a vegetable.

**cumin** This aromatic plant has long, spindly-shaped seeds that can be used either as a condiment or a flavouring. Cumin has a hot and slightly bitter taste.

**curry** Of Indian origin, curry powders are nowadays categorized as mild, hot and very hot, with a wide number of varieties available.

**fever grass** Known in Europe as lemon grass, this plant is versatile and very fragrant. The leaves are used for tea and drinks. The woody stalk is kept for stocks and sauces.

**fricassee** Originating in France, this term relates to various forms of ragoûts (stews) made from meat, fish or vegetables in a white or a brown stock.

**jelly coconut** The young green-shelled coconut that grows into the brown coconut as we know it.

**lemon grass** See Fever grass.

**mango** A large tropical fruit of which there are many varieties. Typically oblong in shape, green when unripe and ripening to a yellow, red or violet colour, mangoes can be used in chutneys or relishes when unripe. When ripe, although it doesn't keep long, it is a wonderful fruit in itself and can be used as a garnish for a wide variety of dishes and salads. Mangoes are soft and sugary with a slightly acidic aftertaste.

**mixed spice** A combination of coriander, cloves, cinnamon, caraway, ginger and pimento, used in puddings, cakes and biscuits.

**nutmeg** Widely used as a spice in cooking, the nutmeg is oval in shape. It is greyish brown in colour and wrinkled in appearance. It has a spicy flavour and aroma and is used grated. As well as being used in cooking for a variety of different dishes, nutmeg can also be used in numerous cocktails and punches.

**okra** Also known as 'ladies' fingers', okra originated in Asia, but was introduced to the Caribbean through Africa. It is used before it is ripe, when it is green and pulpy and the seeds are not completely formed, and is most widely produced as a vegetable.

**ortanique** A cross between an orange and a tangerine, indigenous to Jamaica.

**paprika** This is a spicy seasoning made from a variety of ground sweet red peppers and is best known for its colour.

**parsley** This herb is cultivated mainly for its aromatic leaves and is used as a flavouring or garnish to many dishes. The flat-leaved variety can now be purchased in a wide variety of shops.

**paw-paw** Also known as papaya. In unripe form paw-paw is hard and green, turning a yellow or orange colour when ripe. It is widely used unripe in chutneys and salads, and when fully ripe can be eaten fresh or in a fruit salad and is extremely refreshing.

**pika pepper** A traditional Caribbean sauce, available in supermarkets and shops and mainly used in soups and sauces.

**pimento** A small brown berry, used extensively in Caribbean cooking, with a flavour hinting at cloves, pepper, cinnamon and nutmeg. Also known as allspice.

**plantain** A member of the banana family, larger in fruit and green in colour. Plantains are different from sweet bananas, although they do sweeten the more they ripen, and must always be cooked before eating. Plantain is used widely in Caribbean cooking as a snack or a vegetable.

**poussin** Baby chicken with lots of flavour. Poussin is really succulent and tender.

**red mullet** A lean fish, reddish in colour, the colour being brighter if the fish is scaled as soon as it's caught. The best variety is bright pink streaked with gold. This fish is extremely perishable and must be consumed within a short time of being caught.

**red snapper** A large meaty fish, red in colour. It is favoured for its strong flavour and is readily available at most fishmongers or markets.

**saffron** A spice consisting of the dried stigmas of the saffron crocus. This spice can be purchased in dried form or as an orange-yellow powder. It has a pungent smell and is slightly bitter in taste. Saffron has established itself highly in cookery. It is very expensive, but there are various other substitutes widely available.

**scotch bonnet** The main chilli pepper used in Jamaican cooking. It comes in a variety of colours – green, yellow, orange and brown; green is lower in heat, but still intense in flavour. The other varieties are hotter. Be careful when handling (see Chilli).

**shiso** Known as Japanese mustard cress, shiso has small purple shoots which have a really sweet fragrant flavour.

**strand saffron** Another form of saffron (q.v.).

**sweet potato** Reddish, brown, pink or white on the outside, the flesh of the sweet potato can range from deep orange through to yellow or white in colour. It should be really firm and must have no bruises or smell. It is prepared like a potato and can be used in a variety of dishes, although it is much sweeter. It should always be cooked before eating. Sweet potatoes can be used as a vegetable, as a garnish or as the basis for a dessert. The boniato is the most preferred sweet potato in the Caribbean and is the variety most widely available in Britain.

**thyme** Thyme is one of the basic herbs used in cooking. It is the main savoury herb in Jamaica and is often found in Jamaican markets tied up with a bunch of spring onions as a seasoning package. Thyme contains an essential oil, thymol, which has an extremely aromatic odour. The sprigs can be used fresh or dried and are removed from the dish before serving.

**turmeric** A member of the ginger family, the powdered stem of turmeric is used both as a spice and as a colourant. Turmeric is more bitter in flavour than saffron and is an ingredient found in curry powder.

**watercress**  The most popular form of cress, from the mustard family. It has a distinctive peppery taste and is especially delicious raw, but can also be used cooked. It is available all year round.

# acknowledgements

There are so many people I would like to thank for their support and help throughout the writing of this book.

Special thanks go to my mother for her backing and total faith in me.

Also, thanks to Nick 'Zeus' Wilson, Lindsey Jordan, Edward Bettison, Mark Winwood for his wonderful photographs, Niki Sullivan, Darren Bunn, Etta Wynter and, of course, my number-one fan.

I would like to say a huge thanks to Steve Vella at Daily Fish for supplying me with all the fresh fish and shellfish for the photographs. I apologise for being the biggest pain in the arse in London! Daily Fish are at Unit 12–14, Cedar Way Industrial Estate, Camley Street, London, NW1 0PD and their phone number is 0207-383-3771.

# index

ackee 193
   baked lobster with ackee and okra
      fricassee 81
   fresh saltfish and 75–6
   rouille 162
   and saltfish tartlet 43–4
apple and mango crumble 134
apricots
   roast pumpkin and apricot salad
      with a cumin and pimento
      dressing 30
asparagus
   salad of sweet potato and 29
aubergine 193
   salsa 174
avocados
   baked avocado surprise 59–60
   chicken and guacamole salad
      21
   crab and avocado salad 26

baby back rack 193
   chargrilled 110
baked avocado surprise 59–60
baked beans, fried 7
baked lobster with ackee and okra
      fricassee 81
baked snapper in fragrant spices
      with vegetables 80
balsamic 193
   dressing 184
banana(s)
   cake 140
   fried king fish with fresh
      jangas and boiled green
      74

fruit remedy 3
   sweet banana fritters 125
barbecue sauce 165
   marinating 166
barbecues
   chargrilled baby back rack 110
   charred lobster with garlic butter
      108
   grilled salmon and tuna kebabs
      111
   jerk chicken and pineapple 106
   jerk poussin 112
   pork spare ribs 109
   prawns with chermoula 107
basil 193
batter
   deep-fried squid in curry 86
beans
   blanched French 66
   butter bean soup 18
   French beans with chilli and
      ginger 67
   French beans with red onion,
      coriander and mushrooms
      68
beef
   boiled beef served with island
      vegetables 103–4
   pepperpot soup 16–17
   roast rib eye of 102
beetroot
   roast beetroot with chilli and red
      onion salad 31
belly pork *see* pork
black eye peas salsa 173
blanched French beans 66

blanched spinach 65
boiled beef served with island
    vegetables 103–4
boiled dumplings 37
bread and butter pudding 132
breadfruit, roast 5
breakfast
    cornmeal porridge 10
    fried remedy 4
    fried baked beans 7
    fried plantains 9
    fruit remedy 3
    honey roast ham 8
    roast breadfruit 5
    scrambled eggs 6
bream
    fried 'seasoned' black 77
    roast red bream with chickpeas
        and pea froth 78
bubble and squeak, yam 58
butter
    chilli and coconut 188
    garlic 187
    jerk 186
    melted cabbage 69
butter bean soup 18
butternut squash 193
    dauphinoise 50
    and vegetable curry 49

cabbage
    butter melted 69
    Caribbean coleslaw 33
cakes
    banana 140
    chocolate brownies 135
    Johnny 36
    rum 138–9
callaloo 193
    and poached egg tartlet 45

steamed 63
caramelized pineapple with tamarind
    ice cream 124
Caribbean coleslaw 33
Caribbean crabcake 87
carrot(s)
    christophene and carrot remoulade
        34
    juice 143
    juice punch 144
    purée 56
carrot juice
    Patrick's punch 148
cashew nuts
    jerk chicken with watercress and
        cashew nut dressing 20
casserole
    okra, christophene and plantain
        48
cayenne 193
cerassie 193
    tea 153
champagne
    fresh fruit platter and champagne
        sabayon 126
chargrilled baby back rack 110
chargrilled sweet corn and tomato
    salsa 171
charred lobster with garlic butter
    108
cheese
    macaroni 40
cheesecake, rum and raisin 137
chermoula 193
    barbecued prawns with 107
cherry tomato dressing 183
chicken
    barbecued jerk chicken and
        pineapple 106
    coconut 92

and guacamole salad 21
jerk chicken with watercress and
cashew nut dressing 20
jerk poussin 112
marinated chicken salad with paw-
paw salsa and deep-fried filo
pastry 22–3
roast 93
stew 95–6
chicken livers
stuffing for roast chicken 94
chickpeas 118
roast red bream with chickpeas
and pea froth 78
chillie(s) 193
and coconut butter 188
French beans with chilli and ginger
67
roast beetroot with chilli and red
onion salad 31
Chinese pork 100
chives 193
chocolate
brownies 135
pots 136
christophene(s) 193–4
and carrot remoulade 34
okra, christophene and plantain
casserole 48
and sweet potato 53
chutney, mango 178
cinnamon 194
citrus oyster treats 46
cloves 194
coconut
chicken 92
chilli and coconut butter 188
drops 128
cod
ackee and saltfish tartlet 43–4

fresh saltfish and ackee 75–6
roast fillets of cod with spiced
vegetables 79
coleslaw, Caribbean 33
confit belly pork 99
confit duck legs, roast breast of duck
with 97–8
confit duck salad 24
coriander 194
French beans with red onion,
coriander and mushrooms
68
seared blackened salmon with
a coriander yoghurt dressing
82
corn
chargrilled sweet corn and tomato
salsa 171
cornmeal 194
à la crème 119
porridge 10
sardines in a cornmeal crust with
mixed leaves and pepper frenzy
salsa 83
turned 120
court-bouillon 161
couscous 117
curried shank of lamb with 90
crab
and avocado salad 26
Caribbean crabcake 87
and mango salad 27
and mango salsa 175
cream
cornmeal à la crème 119
crispy leek 62
crumble
apple and mango 134
crumble mixture 133
cucumber juice and mint 155

cumin 194
    roast pumpkin and apricot salad
        with a cumin and pimento
        dressing 30
curried shank of lamb with
    couscous 90
curry 194
    butternut squash and vegetable 49
curry batter
    deep-fried squid in 86
curry oil 190
curry paste 191

deep-fried parsnips 61
deep-fried squid in curry batter 86
dressings
    balsamic 184
    cherry tomato 183
    cumin and pimento 30
    Marie Rose 181
    orange and pink grapefruit 182
    sweet curry vinaigrette 185
    thousand island 180
dried fruit
    rum cake 138–9
drinks
    carrot juice 143
    carrot juice punch 144
    cerassie tea 153
    cucumber juice and mint 155
    guava, mango and orange punch
        150
    Guinness punch 146
    lemon grass tea 154
    mango 151
    Patrick's punch 148
    peanut punch 149
    planters' punch 147
    pumpkin 152
    rum punch 145

sky juice 142
duck
    confit duck salad 24
    roast breast of duck with confit
        duck legs 97–8
dumplings, boiled 37

egg noodles, stir-fried 121
eggs
    callaloo and poached egg tartlet 45
    scrambled 6
    zabaglione Caribbean 127

fever grass 194
fiery oyster salad 25
filo pastry
    marinated chicken salad with paw-
        paw salsa and deep-fried filo
        pastry 22–3
fish
    patties 38–9
    stir-fried egg noodles 121
    stock 159
    *see also* individual names
French beans
    blanched 66
    with chilli and ginger 67
    with red onion, coriander and
        mushrooms 68
fresh fruit platter and champagne
    sabayon 126
fried baked beans 7
fried king fish with fresh jangas and
    boiled green bananas 74
fried plantains 9
fried red mullet with sweet potato
    chips and garlic mayonnaise
    85
fried remedy 4
fried 'seasoned' black bream 77

fritters, sweet banana 125
fruit
    fresh fruit platter and champagne
        sabayon 126
    remedy 3

garlic
    butter 187
    charred lobster with garlic butter
        108
    fried red mullet with sweet potato
        chips and garlic mayonnaise
        85
    mashed potato 54
ginger
    French beans with chilli and 67
    roast plantain soup with fresh
        ginger chantilly 12
grapefruit
    citrus oyster treats 46
    fruit remedy 3
    orange and pink grapefruit
        dressing 182
    pink grapefruit, orange and tomato
        salsa 176
grilled salmon and tuna kebabs
    111
guacamole
    chicken and guacamole salad 21
guava, mango and orange punch
    150
Guinness
    carrot juice punch 144
    punch 146

honey roast ham 8

ice cream
    caramelized pineapple with
        tamarind 124

jangas (king prawns)
    fried king fish with fresh jangas
        and boiled green bananas 74
jelly coconut 194
jerk butter 186
jerk chicken and pineapple,
    barbecued 106
jerk chicken with watercress and
    cashew nut dressing 20
jerk poussin 112
jerk seasoning 177
Johnny cakes 36

kebabs
    grilled salmon and tuna 111
kidney beans
    rice and peas 114
king fish
    fried king fish with fresh jangas
        and boiled green bananas 74
king prawns see jangas

lamb
    curried shank of lamb with
        couscous 90
    lemon and thyme lamb shanks 91
leek, crispy 62
lemon grass tea 154
lemon and thyme lamb shanks 91
lobster
    baked lobster with ackee and okra
        fricassee 81
    charred lobster with garlic butter
        108

macaroni cheese 40
mango 194
    apple and mango crumble 134
    chutney 178
    crab and mango salad 27

mango – *cont.*
    crab and mango salsa 175
    drink 151
mango juice
    guava, mango and orange punch
        150
Marie Rose dressing 181
marinated chicken salad with paw-
        paw salsa and deep-fried filo
        pastry 22–3
marinating barbecue sauce 166
mashed potato 54
mayonnaise 179
meat
    patties 38–9
    stir-fried egg noodles 121
milk
    pumpkin drink 152
    sweet potato pudding 130
mint
    cucumber juice and 155
mixed spice 195
Mornay sauce 163
mullet *see* red mullet
mushrooms
    French beans with red onion,
        coriander and 68

noodles, stir-fried egg 121
nutmeg 195

oil
    curry 190
    pimento 189
okra 195
    baked lobster with ackee and okra
        fricassee 81
    christophene and plantain
        casserole 48
    turned cornmeal 120

onions
    French beans with red onion,
        coriander and mushrooms
        68
    roast beetroot with chilli and red
        onion salad 31
    tomato and onion salad 32
orange juice
    guava, mango and orange punch
        150
    Patrick's punch 148
    planters' punch 147
orange(s)
    citrus oyster treats 46
    and pink grapefruit dressing
        182
    pink grapefruit, orange and tomato
        salsa 176
ortanique(s) 195
    fruit remedy 3
oxtail soup 13–14
oysters
    citrus oyster treats 46
    fiery oyster salad 25

paprika 195
parsley 195
parsnips
    deep-fried 61
pastry
    marinated chicken salad with
        paw-paw salsa and deep-dried
        filo 22–3
    sweet 131
    spiced short 42
Patrick's punch 148
Pat's jerk seasoning 177
Pat's roast chicken 93
patties 38
paw-paws 195

marinated chicken salad with
paw-paw salsa and deep-fried
filo pastry 22–3
peanut punch 149
peas
roast red bream with chickpeas
and pea froth 78
pepper frenzy salsa 172
sardines in a cornmeal crust with
mixed leaves and 83
pepperpot soup 16–17
pickled vegetables 41
pig trotter soup 15
Pika pepper 195
pimento 195
roast pumpkin and apricot salad
with a cumin and pimento
dressing 30
pimento oil 198
pineapple
barbecued jerk chicken and 106
caramelized pineapple with
tamarind ice cream 124
pink grapefruit
orange and pink grapefruit
dressing 182
orange and tomato salsa 176
plantain(s) 195
fried 9
fried remedy 4
mash 55
okra, christophene and plantain
casserole 48
and pumpkin sauce 164
roast plantain soup with fresh
ginger chantilly 12
planters' punch 147
pork
barbecued pork spare ribs 109
chargrilled baby back rack 110

Chinese 100
confit belly pork 99
roast rib of 101
porridge, cornmeal 10
potato(es)
Caribbean crabcake 87
garlic mashed 54
roast 51
see also sweet potatoes
poussin 195
jerk 112

prawns
barbecued prawns with chermoula
107
fried king fish with fresh jangas
and boiled green 74
sautéed 88
puddings
apple and mango crumble 134
bread and butter 132
caramelized pineapple with
tamarind ice cream 124
chocolate brownies 135
chocolate pots 136
coconut drops 128
crumble mixture 133
fresh fruit platter and champagne
sabayon 126
rum and raisin cheesecake
137
spiced rice pudding with raspberry
compote 129
sweet banana fritters 125
sweet potato 130
zabaglione Caribbean 127
pumpkin(s)
drink 152
plantain and pumpkin sauce 164
purée 57

pumpkin(s) – *cont.*
    roast pumpkin and apricot salad
      with a cumin and pimento
      dressing 30
punch
    carrot juice 144
    guava, mango and orange 150
    Guinness 146
    Patrick's 148
    peanut 149
    planters' 147
    rum 145
purée
    carrot 56
    pumpkin 57

raisins
    rum and raisin cheesecake 137
raspberries
    spiced rice pudding with raspberry
      compote 129
red bream
    roast red bream with chickpeas
      and pea froth 78
red kidney beans
    rice and peas 114
red mullet 195–6
    escabeche 84
    fried red mullet with sweet potato
      chips and garlic mayonnaise
      85
red snapper 196
    baked snapper in fragrant
      spices with grilled vegetables
      80
rice
    and peas 114
    seasoned 115
    spiced rice pudding with raspberry
      compote 129

    tomato 116
roast beetroot with chilli and
    red onion salad 31
roast breadfruit 5
roast breast of duck with confit
    duck legs 97–8
roast chicken 93
    stuffing for 94
roast fillets of cod with spiced
      vegetables 79
roast plantain soup with fresh ginger
    chantilly 12
roast potatoes 51
roast pumpkin and apricot salad with
    a cumin and pimento dressing
    30
roast red bream with chickpeas and
    pea froth 78
roast rib eye of beef 102
roast rib of pork 101
rum
    cake 138–9
    planters' punch 147
    punch 145
    and raisin cheesecake 137
    zabaglione Caribbean 127

sabayon
    fresh fruit platter and champagne
    126
saffron 196
salads
    Caribbean coleslaw 33
    chicken and guacamole 21
    christophene and carrot remoulade
    34
    confit duck 24
    crab and avocado 26
    crab and mango 27
    fiery oyster salad 25

jerk chicken with watercress and
cashew nut dressing 20
marinated chicken salad with
paw-paw salsa and deep-fried
filo pastry 22–3
roast beetroot with chilli and red
onion salad 31
roast pumpkin and apricot salad
with a cumin and pimento
dressing 30
sweet potato 28
sweet potato and asparagus 29
tomato and onion 32
salmon
grilled salmon and tuna kebabs
111
seared blackened salmon with a
coriander yoghurt dressing 82
salsas
aubergine 174
black eye peas 173
chargrilled sweet corn and tomato
171
crab and mango 175
paw-paw 22–3
pepper frenzy 172
pink grapefruit, orange and tomato
176
sun-dried tomato 170
sweet potato 168
tomato 169
salt cod
ackee and saltfish tartlet 43–4
saltfish *see* salt cod
sardines in a cornmeal crust with
mixed leaves and pepper frenzy
salsa 83
sauces
ackee rouille 162
barbecue 165

mango chutney 178
marinating barbecue sauce 166
mayonnaise 179
Mornay 163
plantain and pumpkin 164
tomato fondue 167
*see also* dressings; salsas
sautéed prawns 88
sautéed spinach 64
sautéed sweet potatoes 52
Savoy cabbage
Caribbean coleslaw 33
Scotch bonnet 196
scrambled eggs 6
seared blackened salmon with a
coriander yoghurt dressing 82
seasoned rice 115
seasoning
Pat's jerk 177
shellfish
stock 160
shiso 196
sky juice 142
snacks
ackee and saltfish tartlet 43–4
boiled dumplings 37
callaloo and poached egg tartlet
45
citrus oyster treats 46
Johnny cakes 36
macaroni cheese 40
patties 38–9
pickled vegetables 41
snapper
baked snapper in fragrant spices
with grilled vegetables 80
soups
butter bean 18
oxtail 13–14
pepperpot 16–17

soups – *cont.*
  pig trotter 15
  roast plantain soup with fresh
    ginger chantilly 12
spice bag 9, 97, 99, 103, 118, 158
spice rub 95
spiced rice pudding with raspberry
    compote 129
spinach 63
  blanched 65
  sautéed 64
spring greens, stir-fried 70
squash
  butternut squash dauphinoise 50
  butternut squash and vegetable
    curry 49
squid
  deep-fried squid in curry batter 86
steamed callaloo 63
stew chicken 95–6
stir-fried egg noodles 121
stir-fried spring greens 70
stock
  fish 159
  shellfish 160
  vegetable 158
strand saffron 196
stuffing
  for roast chicken 94
summer vegetable tower 71
sun-dried tomato salsa 170
sweet banana fritters 125
sweet corn
  chargrilled sweet corn and tomato
    salsa 171
sweet curry vinaigrette 185
sweet pastry 131
sweet potatoes 196
  christophene and 53
  fried red mullet with sweet potato

  chips and garlic mayonnaise 85
  pudding 130
  salad 28
  salad of sweet potato and
    asparagus 29
  salsa 168
  sautéed 52

tamarind
  caramelized pineapple with
    tamarind ice cream 124
tartlets
  ackee and saltfish 43–4
  callaloo and poached egg 45
  spiced short pastry 42
tea
  cerassie 153
  lemon grass 154
thousand island dressing 180
thyme 196
  lemon and thyme lamb shanks 91
tomato(es)
  chargrilled sweet corn and tomato
    salsa 171
  cherry tomato dressing 183
  fondue 167
  and onion salad 32
  pink grapefruit, orange and tomato
    salsa 176
  rice 116
  salsa 169
  sun-dried tomato salsa 170
tuna
  grilled salmon and tuna kebabs 111
turmeric 196
turned cornmeal 120

vegetables
  baked snapper in fragrant spices
    with grilled 80

boiled beef served with island
  103–4
curry 49
pickled 41
roast fillets of cod with spiced 79
stock 158
summer vegetable tower 71
*see also* individual names
vinaigrette
  sweet curry 185

watercress 197
  jerk chicken with watercress and
    cashew nut dressing 20

yam bubble and squeak 58
yoghurt
  seared blackened salmon with a
    coriander yoghurt dressing 82

zabaglione Caribbean 127